THE SPIRIT OF YELLOWSTONE

THE SPIRIT OF YELLOWSTONE

The Cultural Evolution of a National Park

JUDITH L. MEYER

ROWMAN & LITTLEFIELD PUBLISHERS, INC
Lanham • Boulder • New York • London

ROWMAN & LITTLEFIELD PUBLISHERS, INC.

Published in the United States of America
by Rowman & Littlefield Publishers, Inc.
4720 Boston Way, Lanham, Maryland 20706

3 Henrietta Street
London WC2E 8LU, England

Copyright © 1996 by Rowman & Littlefield Publishers, Inc.

British Cataloging in Publication Information Available

Library of Congress Cataloging-in-Publication Data

Meyer, Judith L., 1956–
The spirit of Yellowstone : the cultural evolution of a national
park / Judith L. Meyer.
p.   cm.
Includes bibliographical references and index.
1. Yellowstone National Park.   2. Man—Influence of environment—
Yellowstone National Park.   I. Title.
F722.M49   1996   978.7'52—dc20   96-15567   CIP

ISBN 0–8476–8248–x (cloth : alk. paper)

Printed in the United States of America

Distributed by NATIONAL BOOK NETWORK

∞ ™ The paper used in this publication meets the minimum requirements of
American National Standard for Information Sciences—Permanence of Paper for
Printed Library Materials, ANSI Z39.48–1984.

CONTENTS

ILLUSTRATIONS

FIGURES

TABLE

ACKNOWLEDGMENTS

A lthough she did not serve as one of the "original sources" referred to in this study, Florence Marguerite Meyer visited Yellowstone National Park as a young woman in 1920, and still, at 101 years of age, her eyes twinkle as she recalls the details of her visit to that special place. Yellowstone memories transcend space and time, binding generations of people to this park, this place. This book is about creating new memories as much as retelling old ones, and it is about the hope that future generations have the chance to experience and appreciate the spirit unique to Yellowstone National Park.

This book could not have been completed without the help of my family—both immediate and extended. To my parents, Edward and Ilse Meyer and Bob and Joan Pavlowsky: thank you for your encouragement, inspiration, and assistance. Thank you for traveling with us when we were children and for making sure we stopped and *knew* a place before moving on. Without you, this project could never have started, progressed, or come to completion. To Aunt Florence and Omi Petersen: thank you for teaching me how important it is to see a place with the heart as well as with the eyes. To Carrie, Aaron, and Johanna: thank you for your patience.

I would like to thank members of the Geography Department at the University of Wisconsin—Madison, including Thomas Vale, Yi-Fu Tuan, Robert Ostergren, David Woodward, and Alan Bogue whose help, continued support, and friendship guided this manuscript.

Others deserve credit for helping this book through its formative years, among them the Yellowstone National Park Archivist, Lee Whittlesey, and the wonderful staff at the Yellowstone Research Library who dropped everything to answer questions and xerox manuscripts. Many thanks go out to Bonnie Sachatello-Sawyer and Joseph Sawyer for their constant encouragement, friendship, and beyond-the-call-of-duty hospitality. A heartfelt "thank you" goes out to Diane Ihle Renkin, too, for providing me with both a job in Yellowstone and a place to stay while this project was brewing.

Further, I wish to thank Lori Morrow and the Montana Historical Society in Helena, Montana, the National Park Service, the Department of the Interior, and the Northern Pacific–Burlington Northern Railroad for the use of photographs and illustrations in their collections. And many thanks are due the Wisconsin Cartographic Laboratory in Madison, Wisconsin, for the map of Yellowstone National Park included here.

I also would like to thank Rhoda Spencer Martin and Joyce Schnepf for all their help and moral support; Jennifer Ruark, the editors, and the anonymous reviewers at Rowman & Littlefield whose advice, insights, and critical reading of this manuscript helped immensely in its completion; the staff and faculty at Carthage College for their support and tireless efforts copying, mailing, and remailing various drafts; and the teachers at Connie's Child Care Center for their attentive and loving care of my children while I worked on this book.

Finally, I want to thank Bob Pavlowsky for persuading me to finish this project, for sharing my love of Yellowstone and geography, and for our family.

INTRODUCTION

In the spring of 1980, I boarded a Yellowstone Park bus in Gardiner, Montana, and, along with twenty or thirty other new park employees, made the bumpy, gear-grinding journey "up the hill" to Mammoth Hot Springs. Along the way, we exchanged names, points of origin, potential destinations within the park, and glances betraying our excitement and great expectations. Some of us would wait tables or carry bags at Lake Hotel, others would join the "maid brigade" at Canyon Village. I would end up in the Old Faithful area as a tour guide. Like many Yellowstone employees, I came to work in the park for just one season, during summer break from school, to see and do something different, to have an adventure while there were still adventures to be had. I had no idea that, like others before me, I would be drawn back to the park again and again. I had no idea how deeply Yellowstone's spirit would touch my soul.

There is something special about Yellowstone, something undescribable—almost eerie—yet very real. It is not only the air, which smells alternately of pine or sulphur depending on where you stand. It is not only the abundance of water—in waterfalls, rivers, lakes, hot springs, and geysers—in an otherwise arid West. Nor is it a particular view, although there are many to choose from: some ugly, some exhilarating, some awe inspiring. It is the spirit of the place, the whole place, that captivates. To describe Yellowstone by listing its qualities is to do the park an injustice. Yellowstone is more than a recording or recitation of elevations, distances, flora and fauna, geological features, and historical structures. Yellowstone is a "place" and as such, the park houses a *genus loci* or spirit of place: an infectious, irresistible force that stirs something within so many of us.

Some seventy years ago, in an attempt to describe the Grand Canyon of the Yellowstone River for his readers, a park visitor wrote:

1

It is not in singling out each crag and pinnacle, or in separating each bright streak of colour from its neighbor and admiring it alone, that one comes to the fullest appreciation of the grandeur and beauty of the canyon. It is rather in being gradually taken possession of by the spirit of the place, an influence that lasts long after you have ceased to look, a feeling far deeper than the transient delight of gazing on a beautiful picture.[1]

This book is about "being taken possession of by the spirit of the place." On one hand, it is an examination of Yellowstone's powerfully evocative, affective, and attractive spirit: the park's ability to move us intellectually, physically, and emotionally. On the other hand, it is an investigation of those taken possession of: the generations of park visitors who, in describing and communicating their experiences to others, created the park as a recognized "place."

Places are more than locations in space. They are the foci of people's attention and concern. For some, the very name of a place can conjure up sights, sounds, smells, even the *feel* of that place. And, just as individual people have personalities—some more endearing, complex, or interesting than others—so do individual places have personalities. "A place is nothing in itself," wrote Wallace Stegner. "It has no meaning, it can hardly be said to exist, except in terms of human perception, use, and response."[2] If this is true, Yellowstone as place is a human artifact. Our shared perception of the place is the product of people interacting with, being influenced by, and assigning meanings to its landscape.

In many ways, this book is a response to those who have written about Yellowstone in recent years emphasizing how it has changed, pointing out how it has succumbed to human intrusion and impacts, and lamenting how it is failing us somehow. The assumption inherent in these observations is that the park is not what it should be: an example of pristine Nature or a symbol of our altruistic—rather than economic, scientific, or political—concern for wild nature. However, as a "place," rather than as a "national park," there is much that has *not* changed about Yellowstone. Humans have indeed intruded upon and have had an impact on the park, but this place has had an equally powerful impact on us. And, it may be we, through our insensitivity to the park's qualities as place, who are failing the park.

In closing this introduction, I defer once again to one who preceded me into Yellowstone. In a book entitled *Your Western National Parks*, a former park ranger wrote:

Before leaving Yellowstone I feel that a word is in order regarding what I like to term the *spirit* of the place. With all due respect to other national parks, there is a spirit here that is found nowhere else. It is a spirit born of tradition. Started, perhaps, by the old-time stage drivers that swung their teams over the early roads, or by the guides of forty years ago who originated tall tales of the park phenomena, it is carried on season after season by those who work in Yellowstone during the summer.[3]

Each of the national parks—every place that has meant something to someone—is haunted by a unique spirit of our making. Each of the great nature parks is steeped in tradition and rich in history, beauty, and wildness. Each one touches us individually and as a nation and therefore deserves our attention, concern, and compassion. However, for me, one park stands out from the rest. In Yellowstone, I have heard the siren's call.

1

REVOLUTIONARY IDEAS AND EVOLUTIONARY PROCESSES

On 1 March 1872, Yellowstone National Park was established as the world's first national park. Its enabling act was entitled "The National Park," because, like "the" sun or "the" moon, its uniqueness allowed the singular distinction. Today, there are 369 units within the U.S. National Park System—more than 50 of them nature parks—and all are administrative progeny of that first national park. But why was the Yellowstone region chosen as the site of such a novel and revolutionary idea? Some suggest the region's geographical isolation was enough to cause its removal from the public domain just a decade after the Homestead Act was passed. Others would have us believe it was the strange geological and hydrothermal features that prompted protection but not without an eye toward Yellowstone's potential as a tourist attraction. Perhaps the creation of The National Park had very little to do with geography, politics, or economics at all. Perhaps it was a chance event—the culmination of a history of attempts on the part of the nation to preserve wild, scenic, and interesting places.[1]

Since its establishment, Yellowstone National Park has matured into a national and international symbol of our desire to protect and preserve natural landscapes. Its history parallels in time and spirit the development of the idea of national parks as well as the birth and maturation of the National Park Service (NPS) as a governing agency devoted to nature protection. And, among park historians, it is common practice to refer to Yellowstone's "evolution" as well as the "evolution" of the national park idea or the "evolution" of the National Park Service. For example, Alfred Runte, an authority on national park history, states that "the national park idea as we know it today did not emerge in finished form. More accurately, it evolved."[2] In writing about Yellowstone National Park specifically, W. Turrentine Jackson said,

"The idea of establishing a national park . . . was the result of an evolutionary process."[3] Hence, the term "evolution" is commonly relied upon to describe the developmental history of the national parks both collectively and individually. Further, this evolutionary process is typically characterized as a reflection of our evolving relationship toward nature more generally. As our attitudes toward nature change, so do—or so should—our attitudes toward the national parks.

It is this line of thinking that has caused the National Park Service continually to adapt its management philosophies and policies to keep pace with changing views of nature and "reflect ongoing evolution in public taste."[4] As a result, there has been little consistency over the years in park management. One park historian believes that "the Park Service no longer knows what its purpose is nor that of the Park System it manages."[5] In recent times, as part of a national "back to nature" movement begun in the 1960s, NPS management has been based on achieving and maintaining some illusion, if not actual state, of wildness in the parks. As part of this "keep it natural" philosophy, the Service uses science in the form of ecosystems management or ecosystems restoration to guide its management programs. However, national parks are more than representative bits of wild nature. They are deeply humanized landscapes, endowed with meanings beyond those associated solely with their value as ecosystems. And, people's affection for particular parks as "places" tends to withstand broader societal changes in attitudes toward nature more generally. In other words, people's expectations of a visit to Yellowstone, or Yosemite, or Grand Canyon National Parks are not necessarily based only on those individuals' attitudes toward nature as a concept. Instead, the public's expectations of an individual park experience are related to that park's personality, its image, which has developed in that place over time. Given the current NPS management philosophy, however, conflicts can, and often do, arise between what the public has come to expect of a particular park experience and the Park Service's new and ever-changing ideas about nature and natural systems.

MODELS OF EVOLUTION

Evolution—whether the biological evolution of a species or the cultural evolution of a national park—implies change. But evolution is not uncontrolled, unconditional change. If changes are to be described as "evolutionary," then they must proceed within the limits of an ancestral form and within certain constraints. The punctuated equilibrium model of biological evolution first introduced by Stephen Jay Gould and Niles Eldridge is especially useful as a framework or model for understanding the cultural evolution of national parks. Briefly, the punctuated equilibrium model states that species exist for long periods of time undergoing relatively little change. This is the "equilibrium" stage, a period of stasis and stability. Then, eventually, a chance event occurs, the "punctuation," which brings about changed environmental conditions favoring the selective survival of some individuals and some species over others.[6] What makes this model attractive to the study of national parks is the model's emphasis on stasis. It can be argued that it is during the long periods of stasis that a national park develops a unique character or personality. It is over long periods of time that a park becomes familiar to and beloved by the public.

Generally, such periods of stasis have been overlooked in the writings by national park historians and scholars in favor of the seemingly more exciting and controversial—hence more newsworthy—episodes of change: changes in national attitudes toward nature, changes in national park policies, and physical changes within the parks themselves. Of main concern in most national park histories are the watershed decisions or dramatic events, which altered the course of national park policy.[7] By focusing on change, national park history has typically been described as a series of steps or eras, wherein each era is associated with a prevalent societal, political, or scientific trend.[8] Such work is important and necessary to our understanding of the national parks. However, this perspective presents only part of the picture. By looking at the history of the national parks only for evidence or proof of correlation between changing attitudes toward nature and changing purposes of the national parks, trends other than those that fit the authors' specific chronologies have been overlooked. One such trend is the existence of a persistent sense or spirit of place. Despite changes in administrations, governing philosophies, and land and resource management practices over the past one-and-a-quarter centuries, there is much about Yellowstone that has not changed.

Along with calling attention to what has not changed, three further components of the punctuated equilibrium model provide insight into our understanding of national park history. First is the importance of initial conditions in influencing subsequent development. Origins are important because they set the stage for all that follows. Second is the idea that evolutionary change occurs as a process of elaboration rather than elimination. Over time, evolution proceeds along lines of both diversity and specialization. As a framework for national park evolution, the punctuated equilibrium model might encourage us to consider that the meanings we attribute to individual national parks over time do not change from one thing to another so much as these meanings become richer, more profound, and more specific to both public needs and the constraints of the individual park's physical landscape. Third and finally is the misconception of the ideal. Entities—whether a particular individual, species, or a particular park—are part of a larger continuum driven not by progress toward some higher, ideal state but by historical contingency and chance. When a national park is first conceived in the collective national consciousness, it is an entity in its own right, a unique place, not a tendency toward some ideal. Taken together, these four elements of biological evolution theory provide new insight into understanding the cultural evolution of charismatic places like Yellowstone National Park.

In Yellowstone, over recent decades, the general public as well as constituents of particular political and scientific communities have voiced criticisms concerning the changeable nature of Yellowstone's management policies. Whether the topic is the fate of Yellowstone's grizzlies, the merits of a "free burn" forest-fire policy, or the value of wolf reintroduction, Yellowstone's management strategies often seem mired in controversy. Currently, Yellowstone is being managed so as to provide an experience of nature rather than of place. And, as public attitudes change, so must Park Service management. Such a guiding philosophy leaves little room for nurturing and maintaining the integrity of the park's sense of place, something sorely and increasingly lacking not only in Yellowstone but in other grand old parks, the "crown jewels" of the national park system. As Yellowstone's superintendent stated after the 1988 summer of wildfires, the NPS's management program is an "uneasy truce between what science tells us is possible and what our value system tells us is appropriate."[9] Adopting a new perspective on the evolution of the national parks—one that releases park management, in part, from society's changing attitude toward nature and acknowledges the importance of people's affection for parks as places—may resolve some of the criticism aimed at the NPS and bring about a new appreciation for the national parks.

YELLOWSTONE'S WRITTEN RECORD

To date, thousands of articles, books, pamphlets, and government reports on the Yellowstone region have been written, and the number grows every year as more people visit the park and record their impressions.[10] Similarly, the large number of poems, paintings, sketches, even photographs and musical scores that have been produced in an effort to describe and honor the place attest to its evocative nature. Many of these materials have been employed in the writing of several good Yellowstone histories.[11] However, these descriptive materials have typically been used selectively to support or illustrate a chronology of events or trends, usually with political or personal undertones.[12] In such works, a structure is imposed on the park's history and the literature that supports the particular author's classification scheme and time line. Park historians thereby focus attention not on the place, the original authors, or the specific language in the various accounts but on their own expectations. In this study, Yellowstone's written record was approached not as a collection of anecdotal material to be used only in support of theories born outside of the literature but as a coherent body of information or data in its own right.

The ideas presented here regarding the evolution and persistence of a distinct spirit of place for Yellowstone National Park are the result of a study of Yellowstone literature spanning the 121 years of park history between 1870 and 1991.[13] Since the first generations of park tourists were predominantly responsible for creating meanings and assigning them to the newly established park, it seemed only fitting to draw heavily from these early accounts.[14] And, since a goal of this study was to identify and substantiate the existence of Yellowstone's sense of place—the sort experienced by the general public— rather than identifying management goals or other hidden agendas, tourist accounts comprised the largest proportion of sources used. Included as well were federal government documents such as survey and expedition reports, park superintendents' reports, rangers' field notes, and later, circulars and notices published by the Department of the Interior and the National Park Service. In the first decade of the park's establishment, the reports of Ferdinand Hayden figured heavily, since his expeditions to the park in 1871, 1872, and 1878 led to the publication of a wide variety of materials. State government publications promoting tourism and settlement in the surrounding states of Montana, Wyoming, and Idaho were included, as were pamphlets and books published by park concessioners, railroad promoters, and travel agencies. In addition, special attention was paid to the content and format of guidebooks, since such publications have enjoyed both high and continuous popularity among park-goers.

In all accounts, the experiences described by employees were compared with those of visitors, locals with those who traveled great distances, and the wealthy with the less well off. Surprisingly, little variation was found in these various authors' descriptions of the park experience. Overwhelmingly, authors of the earliest accounts describing Yellowstone were predominantly male, a reflection of the times rather than literary biases. Most of Yellowstone's early tourists, reporters, and surveyors were indeed men. Every attempt was made to include women's accounts, but the fact remains that fewer women than men visited the park in its early years, and fewer women than men left written records of their visits during this time.

Unlike many of the topics now open to reinterpretation by current revisionist thinking in the study of American history, the idea that there are or were differences in men's and women's impressions of Yellowstone does not stand out in the literature. Both sexes apparently took part in typical tourist activities and registered similar reactions. However, diaries and notations of camp life as well as some of the earliest photographs of Yellowstone's tourists indicate that women continued to perform household chores and care for children while en route through the park, whereas men more than women engaged in hunting and fishing activities. Hence, although men and women saw the same sights and responded in similar ways to the Yellowstone landscape, their daily routines did differ.[15]

The Yellowstone literature was then evaluated as a whole, as an entity capable and worthy of investigation, in the hopes of discovering underlying patterns. What was found was that along with repeated descriptions of particular locations within the park, six themes appeared consistently and prominently in the literature: (1) the beauty or aesthetic qualities of the landscape; (2) the uniqueness of the place; (3) tourism and recreation; (4) the park as a wilderness; (5) the democratic nature of the park experience; and (6) the park as a place for education (see photographs 1–4).

Beauty: "No greater work of art"

Almost all Yellowstone accounts make mention in some way of the aesthetic qualities of the park landscape, whether that landscape is a particular scene, a sweeping panoramic view, or the park as a whole. This aesthetic, visual component is commented on more often in the Yellowstone literature than references to any other aspect of a Yellowstone experience (figure 1.1). Park visitors seem to have a well-trained sense of what is pleasing to the eye, and comments such as the following are common: "The view from this point

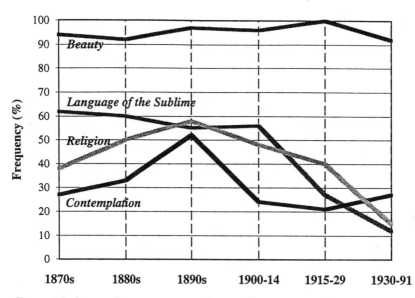

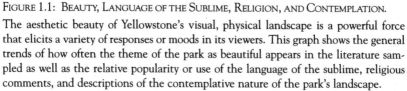

FIGURE 1.1: BEAUTY, LANGUAGE OF THE SUBLIME, RELIGION, AND CONTEMPLATION.
The aesthetic beauty of Yellowstone's visual, physical landscape is a powerful force that elicits a variety of responses or moods in its viewers. This graph shows the general trends of how often the theme of the park as beautiful appears in the literature sampled as well as the relative popularity or use of the language of the sublime, religious comments, and descriptions of the contemplative nature of the park's landscape.

was one of the fairest that I have ever gazed upon. It seemed to unite all the elements of beauty—hill, grassy plains, and winding streams."[16]

Much of the language used in the late 1800s to describe the park as beautiful can also be found in writings describing other national parks or nature resorts during that same period and is common to the description of nature as sublime. The idea of nature as sublime describes a human response that combines an appreciation for aesthetic beauty with physical danger or fear.[17] In *Niagara Falls: Icon of the American Sublime*, Elizabeth McKinsey identifies a score of literary devices that characterize the language of the sublime in early American nature writing. Among others, she includes: (1) the use of romantic and classical terms in the naming of natural features; (2) the use of superlatives and hyperbole; (3) the stringing-together of adjectives so as to create a sensation of being overwhelmed by the visual scene; (4) an admonition of speechlessness or inability to describe properly the scene often accompanied by comparisons to works of art; (5) the use of specific words such as "gloomy," "grandeur," "majesty," "picturesque," and "sublime"; and (6) references to God or natural forces beyond human understanding that reveal the insignificance and powerlessness of humans.

However, although the idea of nature as sublime was a popular literary movement of the eighteenth and nineteenth centuries, it lingers on in Yellowstone accounts well into the twentieth century. On the one hand, this may reflect merely an attachment to the traditional and familiar or the use of literary conventions. On the other hand, it may also suggest that references to the sublime were, for many people for a long time, the best means of describing what they really felt: an insignificance or reverence in the presence of nature or God, an inability to describe accurately the beauty of the scene, or a sense of being moved—often to the point of being physically overwhelmed—by the visual scene.

According to Yellowstone accounts, the park's aesthetic qualities lie not only in majestic, sublime, and dramatic landscapes but also in the more commonplace: "Not only are there scores of grand mountains lifting their craggy sides and rugged summits (few of which have ever felt the tread of civilized man) far up among the clouds, but innumerable sunny glades and shady dells, charming bits of quiet, picturesque scenery, where one will see nothing of the striking, but only the gently beautiful."[18] The park's spectacular scenery moves and inspires its viewers, but the simple and lovely charm of the place touches them as well. Particular mention is made of the classic beauty of Yellowstone Lake with its panoramic views of distant mountains, watery expanse, and endless shoreline. This soothing scene is then juxtaposed with the almost overpowering beauty of the Grand Canyon and the exhilarating beauty of the geyser basins.

Whether in its grand displays or more mundane views, the beauty of the Yellowstone landscape often fosters contemplation or pensive or reflective moments. Tourists write that they "would go forth to spend another day in contemplation of the wondrous works of the Great Creator."[19] Comments describing religious contemplation or inspiration commonly appear alongside attempts to describe the park's beauty, such as in a diary entry that reads, "I thank God for creating such scenery and again for permitting my eyes to behold it."[20] Such comments should be expected, however, since the language of the sublime has strong religious ties. However, the park's scenery elicits religious comments that are not necessarily associated with the sublime. There are many instances of quoting from Scripture, singing of hymns, or referring explicitly or implicitly to a Supreme Being as in this description of the Mammoth Hot Springs: "Just below the large spring . . . is a grove of good-sized pines nearly buried in the sediment, while back of this, up the mountainside where abound the caves and fissures . . . not a half-mile away, are trees a hundred years old, growing on the same formation. Known unto the Great Architect, and to him only, are all his works. His ways are past finding out."[21]

Further, not all contemplative activity is religious. For the Earl of Dunraven, author of *The Great Divide*, a book that familiarized much of England with Yellowstone and the American West, the view from atop Mount Washburn is inspiring in an educational sense:

> It is pleasant thus to gaze out upon the world from some lofty standpoint. . . . It seems to expand the mind; it conducts one by easy pathways down long lands of thought penetrating far into the future of nations, and opens out broad vistas of contemplation through which glimpses of what may be can dimly be discerned. The outlook from such a commanding point elevates the mind, and the soul is elated by the immensity of Nature.[22]

Hence, the theme of contemplation appears in many forms: intellectual, moral, and personal as well as religious: "Looking 'through Nature up to Nature's God' can be done easily in this 'Wonderland,' and the overwhelming influence may help one to live better all his life. . . . All of its impressions are grand and enobling in the highest degree,—just the inspiring elements which lift the soul into honor, and beget lofty aims."[23]

For some, the park's beauty instigates quiet, soul-searching contemplation while in others it instigates a desire for scientific investigation or a seemingly forgotten sense of youthful curiosity. As one tourist wrote of the geyser eruptions, "It was all most wonderful and intensely interesting, giving rise to theories, conjectures, and strange thoughts."[24] For many, just being on vacation and seeing new and different sights encourages contemplation. "I spent one of the most profitable hours of my life," writes Alma White while visiting Yellowstone's Upper Falls. "Surrounded by nature in all its primitive beauty and grandeur, I forgot my burdens."[25]

Contemplation, as a category by itself, is most likely underrepresented graphically, since it accompanies and is incorporated into other responses. Religion and contemplation are both more subtle, private, and personal responses, and perhaps for this reason, too, they do not appear as often in the literature. A religious or spiritual element is still evident today in Yellowstone accounts but is tempered with the more secular language and attitudes of modern times.

The Unique: "One imagines that he is no longer in the same country."

Second only to an appreciation for the aesthetic beauty of the Yellowstone landscape is a delight in its uniqueness: the novelty and wonder of this particular place (figure 1.2). This theme should not be construed as descriptive of a simple fascination for "singularities," which was part of the attraction of the sublime. Instead, uniqueness describes an appreciation for something unique to Yellowstone as place with a spirit or sense of place all its own: "Those who may hereafter visit this strange land will bear me out in asserting that a peculiar sensation takes possession of the visitor which can not be dispelled."[26]

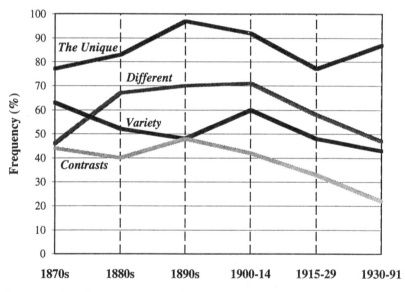

FIGURE 1.2: THE UNIQUE, DIFFERENT, VARIETY, AND CONTRASTS.

In this graph, the frequency of comments describing the park as unique is shown over time as well as three variations on the idea of the unique. First, Yellowstone is unique because it is unusual. Second, the park is composed of a unique variety of features. Finally, Yellowstone is unique because of the odd combinations or contrasts to be found juxtaposed in the park's landscape—hot and cold springs, green meadows and lifeless geyser basins, quiet hot springs and boisterous geysers.

Descriptions of the park's uniqueness fall into many categories. One is that Yellowstone is unique because it is so strange, so very different from the landscapes with which most people are familiar. Yellowstone's landscape is uncommon, unusual, and contains "objects more stupendous than the imagination had ever pictured."[27] Especially with their first view of the geyser basins, people admit disbelief and astonishment: "Sitting on our horses we gazed and gazed in silent wonderment at the outstretched world below."[28]

Another aspect of Yellowstone's uniqueness is the variety of its wonders: "Thousands have visited it yearly and have been impressed by the wide range of the phenomena found there. This is one of its great peculiarities. It is, so to speak, many sided in its character. . . . Within a space of about 3,344 square miles [Nature] has concentrated such a variety of objects as one would only expect to find scattered throughout the universe."[29] One Yellowstone guidebook points out all the contrasts to be found in just a single thermal area: "An anomalous feature of this wonderful hot spring system is that pools of different colors lie in closest proximity, each spring being independent of the other, having varying levels at the surface, as well as varying temperatures and pulsations."[30] Another author describes the variety and contrasts of the Fountain Paint Pot area:

> Its whole surface is pitted with holes, large and small, in which hot water bubbles and growls, grunts and roars, in every tone of the gamut. Some of the pools are black, others white, and others yellow with sulphur. A choice variety of odors is also observable. . . . In this neighborhood hot and cool pools lay side by side, presenting the most astonishing contrast. Why one stream of water should be boiling while another two feet from it is cold, is difficult to explain.[31]

Not just the thermal areas, but the whole park is a study of contrasts. Stark western peaks rise from "such shady places as fringe the old pastures on the New England hills."[32] In the interior of the park, wide and colorful canyons give way downstream to dark and narrow defiles. At the park's higher elevations, alpine meadows are carpeted with wildflowers and large forests with thick stands of fir, spruce, and pine.

Within this variety are the park's strange contrasts or juxtapositions. Yellowstone is "a place where there is beauty and ugliness everywhere, peace and chaos, the pastoral and the sublime."[33] Earlier tourists, especially, saw the park as a "rare, multifarious collection of curious and countless samples . . .

placed side by side . . . the fair and the foul, the simple and grand, the lovely and revolting, the colossal and the fairy form, and the terrifying and the delightful."[34] Whether simply another allusion to Yellowstone as the dwelling place of spirits and demons or a comment on the ultimate of contrasts, Yellowstone is for many "ein Bild der Wunder und der Schrecken,"[35] a picture of wonder and horror, situated in a unique position between Heaven and Hell.

Tourism: "What a playground for a nation!"

From the time of its inception, Yellowstone National Park was to be a place for tourists. In its enabling act, Yellowstone was proposed to be a public park or pleasuring ground as well as a nature preserve. And, as a result, almost every activity undertaken in the park—from reading the newspaper in the Old Faithful Inn to backcountry hiking—is considered by many to be a tourist activity (figure 1.3). For the park's earliest tourists, one of Yellowstone's unique attractions was its supposedly therapeutic hot spring water, and the public's perception of the park as a health resort was popular for three decades. Tourists were lured to Yellowstone to "take the cure" by soaking in and drinking the hot spring water and relaxing at the park's various luxury hotels.

The park's first promoters popularized an image of Yellowstone as a place to cure various ailments. The hot waters, especially, had a reputation for restorative powers: "Around them had already gathered a number of invalids, who were living in tents, and their praises were enthusiastic in favor of the sanitary effects of the springs. Some of them were used for drinking and others for bathing purposes."[36] Yellowstone's hot springs were repeatedly touted as cures for rheumatism and skin diseases, until they were scientifically proven to have no therapeutic value. Then, promoters focused attention on the invigorating and rejuvenating qualities of the park's high elevation and local climate, which "cannot be surpassed in the world for its health-giving powers."[37] Included, as well, was the "pure, bracing air, free from fog."[38] Tourists, however, quickly noted the difference between invigoration and shortness-of-breath and, good-naturedly, commented accordingly: "The hotel which we had just left is 6,500 feet above sea-level, but we immediately began to climb to a greater altitude, and soon became aware of the fact that we were getting up in the world."[39]

Despite the fact that Yellowstone's popularity as a health resort diminished quickly after the turn of the century, many people went—and continue to go—to Yellowstone hoping to take part in activities that are presumably

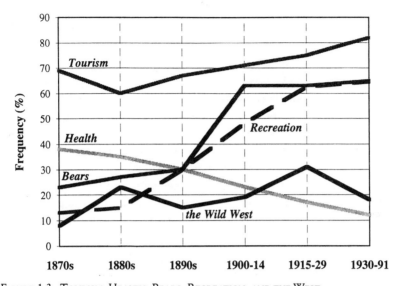

FIGURE 1.3: TOURISM, HEALTH, BEARS, RECREATION, AND THE WEST.
Tourism is consistently most popular compared with the themes listed here, but it is only slightly more popular than recreation by the 1990s. Traveling to Yellowstone for one's health was second only to tourism when the park was first established, but comments attributing visits to the park for health reasons decrease steadily over time. Generally bears are mentioned as often as recreation in the park's more recent history. There is little change over the years in the popularity of the idea of Yellowstone as part of the Wild West experience. It is a lower-priority theme but persistent nonetheless.

healthy because they are undertaken in the out-of-doors. Whether the purpose of the trip is a day hike, a picnic with the family, a backcountry expedition, or to photograph wildlife, tourists flock to Yellowstone to be in the Great Outdoors. If one interprets these activities as being a form of stress release or health-conscious decision, these modern outdoor recreationists are—in many ways—following the footsteps of earlier Yellowstone "outpatients."

In the literature of Yellowstone's earliest decades, it is easier to distinguish between tourism and (outdoor) recreation than it is today. Over time, these two purposes for visiting the park have become inseparably linked. "Tourism" assumes there is some form of travel for the participant. He or she travels from "home," and, both en route and at the destination or destinations, engages in activities that are not standard fare back home. These activities may be arranged specifically for tourists but not necessarily. "Recreation" can be undertaken at home and away and assumes there is some diversion from the norm that allows the mind and/or body to be restored or rejuvenated. Tourists often engage in activities that are both forms of tourism and recreation, such as participating in a nature hike. The act of walking may be recreational, but the idea of traveling to a place that has been set up specifically for visitors to come and hike makes the activity a form of tourism as well. For many, the act of traveling itself, being "on the road," constitutes tourism regardless of whether there is an actual destination or destinations. By the 1900s, describing Yellowstone's purpose in terms of providing recreational activities is almost as common as describing it in terms of tourism. Today, people's perception of what constitutes national park recreation can vary from dangerous, life-threatening, or endurance-testing experiences to viewing a park's features from the window of an air-conditioned touring coach. Nevertheless, all such activities, if undertaken in a national park, seemingly constitute some form of tourism.

Other aspects of the tourism-recreation theme emerge from Yellowstone's literature. For some, Yellowstone is a remnant or vestige of the American frontier, and tourists are encouraged to relive the myth of the Wild West. In the following, the author hopes to convince tourists to enter Yellowstone from Cody, Wyoming, by invoking images of Buffalo Bill: "As you pass the memorial statue erected in [Buffalo Bill's] honor you rejoice in the reality that the West to which he belonged—the West of bison, of wild game, of stream and plain and mountain—is not a thing of the past but lives on perpetually amid the magical splendors of Yellowstone Park, preserved unspoiled always, for the benefit and enjoyment of the people."[40]

Still today, the popularity of tourist activities such as stagecoach and horseback rides and chuckwagon cookouts attest to people's perception of the park as a place to re-create Wild West days. However, these activities are not so much a part of Yellowstone's sense of place as they are a more general experience of the American West. This is shown in the relatively consistent but low popularity of typical Wild West activities in the park as opposed to the rapidly growing popularity of seeing or looking for bears. Grizzly bears, certainly, play a major role in people's expectations of a trip to Yellowstone, and many people think of the bears as a tourist attraction. However, Yellowstone's grizzlies are representative of more than one theme in the Yellowstone literature. They may be tourist attractions to some, but for others, the Yellowstone grizzly is an indicator of the park's ecological health, its wildness, and its integrity as a wildlife preserve.

Wilderness: "The gravel in the crop of civilization that aids digestion of the whole"

The theme of Yellowstone National Park as a wilderness is well represented in the literature (figure 1.4) both in its own right and as a broad, all-encompassing theme, since "wilderness" is a word rich in meanings of its own, especially for Americans. From the literature, a sense of the public's respect for the park's wildness or naturalness emerges, and the very size of the park—its vastness—is a part of that wildness. Although millions of tourists pass through the park each summer, individuals write of the park's wilderness setting as if coveting its solitude. Hence, the park's wilderness qualities can be appreciated on a variety of levels. On one hand, Yellowstone National Park truly is a wilderness. To say its purpose as a national park is to preserve

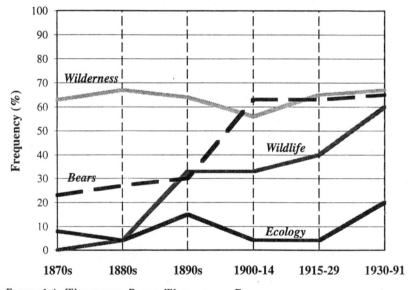

FIGURE 1.4: WILDERNESS, BEARS, WILDLIFE, AND ECOLOGY.

Yellowstone today is an icon of the wilderness movement. However, the park's historical record suggests that the park's wilderness qualities have always been appreciated. Bears—whether beggar bears that used to line the roads or the elusive Yellowstone grizzlies of today—have always been a unique Yellowstone attraction, but the number of comments describing bears has risen sharply since the 1890s when it eclipsed the number of comments describing Yellowstone wildlife more generally. The idea of Yellowstone as an ecologically intact wilderness is not new to the most recent decades. Instead, the park's written record shows that an ecological conscience has existed since the park's inception.

wilderness would be redundant: much of the park is a wilderness. On the other hand, Yellowstone is a symbol of wilderness or an icon of sorts for wilderness preservationists. Yellowstone is a shrine or sacred place for wilderness enthusiasts, an almost religious aspect of this theme: "Long may the American people have a tract of country that is not cut up by railroads, telegraph and telephone poles, and given over into the hands of railroad kings. . . . Let the American people fear to desecrate this place, or dedicate it to low and avaricious purposes."[41] The grizzly, the native cutthroat trout, the wolf, the bison, and Old Faithful Geyser are all nationally recognized symbols of Yellowstone's wildness, but all signify different motivations or topics of concern within the wilderness movement.

Often, Yellowstone's wilderness is described in association with nationalistic statements that credit our democratic form of government for the preservation of Yellowstone's wildness: "It is the wildness and grandeur of the enclosing mountain scenery . . . that have raised it to sudden fame, and caused it to be set apart by our national government as a grand national play-ground . . . free to all men for all time."[42] The public applauds the government's decision not only to remove the park from private ownership but also to continually reassert its claim that Yellowstone is a *nation's* park: "The Government continues to adhere to its original policy of maintaining forever so far as possible the virgin splendor of the people's great playground. In this it must now and always will have the support and approval of enlightened and patriotic people of every nation."[43]

Yet another wilderness subtheme is Yellowstone's purpose as a wildlife preserve: "Geysers are startling, weird, spectacular; the colors of the boiling springs are marvelous; the gay yellows and reds of the strange soft-rocked canyon are exciting; but Yellowstone excited us most of all as a lovely bit of mountain wilderness, where elk and moose and beaver; bison and antelope and mountain sheep, seemed to live as they had lived in pre-Columbian days."[44] However, concern for the park's wildlife does not appear in historical accounts during the park's first few decades, probably since wildlife was still considered a culinary treat as much as a visual one, and because wildlife was plentiful throughout the western states. The popularity of viewing wildlife in its natural, unfenced setting really only becomes popular after the turn of the century. Today, it is a major reason for visiting the park.

In Yellowstone, the grizzly bear is not only a form of park wildlife. For some, grizzlies epitomize the real wildness and danger of a true wilderness: "One of the most important parts of the grizzly country experience, besides its rareness, is that hackle-raising humility that comes from knowing one is in the presence of a superior predator. Of knowing that one is, for once, a potential prey species. I hope we never reach the point where we are not allowed to have that feeling."[45] The author adds, however, that "being mauled by a grizzly bear has always struck me as one of those wilderness experiences where the novelty wears off almost right away."[46]

The grizzlies' presence in Yellowstone nowadays is considered proof of Yellowstone's wildness, and the size of the park's bear population is often used as an indicator of Yellowstone's ecological health. However, threads of ecological thought have always been present in people's perceptions of the park although not in such numbers as wilderness proponents of today might wish. Ecology appears in the park's written record as an early and sustained theme that suggests that people have long recognized ecological principles and the need to protect entire ecosystems. In the following, the author describes the so-called parks or open valleys between mountains, and, although it reveals an anthropocentric view of nature, the passage does attest to an awareness of ecological interdependence: "They are not only beautiful but useful, and answer a very wise purpose in the economy of Nature, for, acting like huge reservoirs, they collect the thousand rills that steal out from under the everlasting snows, and uniting them in one perennial stream launch it out into the world to bear fertility to the arid plains below."[47]

Although sophisticated knowledge of the ecological links between different species and between biological species and their physical environments were not known a century ago, people were aware of the "interconnectedness" of the natural world. Early accounts tell of the need to protect not only Yellowstone's forests but those of the regions surrounding the park. And, people understood the park's value not only as wildlife habitat but as reservoir: "The whole region is covered with a thick forest growth cutting off the intense rays of the summer sun, and covering the ground with a vegetable mold through which the surface waters filter but slowly. It is a conservative estimate . . . that these forests prolong the melting of the snows from four to six weeks."[48]

The current dilemma of reconciling the ideals of wilderness preservation with the realities of tourism is not a new one and has roots deep in Yellowstone's past. People have always expressed both approval and disappointment in the management of the park's wilderness areas. In general, however, much of Yellowstone's public is satisfied with the park's gentrified wilderness:

It is hardly safe in these days to define a wilderness, it contains so much that is unexpected. We must refuse to be convinced by the unsatisfied one who finds incongruity in the ugly red hotels, the yellow coaches, the galloping tourists, the kodaks. After all, every age is entitled to its own sort of wilderness, and ours seems to include the tourist and the hotel; the traveler is to-day as much a part of the Rocky Mountains as the elk or the lodgepole pine. No picture of the modern wilderness would to-day be complete without the sturdy gold-skirted American girl with her kodak, the whitetop wagon, the Eastern youth turned suddenly Western, with oddly worn sombrero and spurs.[49]

Most people believe that nature and people can and should coexist in the park, if only because of Yellowstone's great size. Yellowstone's written record suggests that there is room enough for both wilderness purists and those who enjoy a more civilized wilderness experience:

Behind us lay a week of luxurious sight-seeing in Yellowstone Park—the civilized part of it, thick with hotels, camps, and campers, autos and tourists. Before us lay alluring weeks of the open trail in the country to the south, within the Park and out of it—a blessed country of no roads, and few visitors. An undisturbed fairyland of mountains, rivers and forests, all populated with wild life like a vast unfettered zoo.[50]

Democracy: "Maintained by the Nation for the people"

Yellowstone tourists have persistently included statements in their narratives that describe their feelings of pride in the American government for its role in establishing Yellowstone National Park, and "democracy" rather than "nationalism" may more aptly describe these feelings. Evidence of nationalism—as it has been used in recent scholarly debates over the evolution of the parks—is found in expressions of nationalistic pride that compare the United States to other countries. In Yellowstone's historic, literary record, nationalistic comments appear more frequently than comments telling of the benefits of a democratic government or the democratic nature of park tourists (figure 1.5). However, in American nature writing of the late 1800s and especially in the promotional materials associated with the opening of the American West, nationalistic references are common literary devices and are not necessarily pro-American or antiforeign in intent.

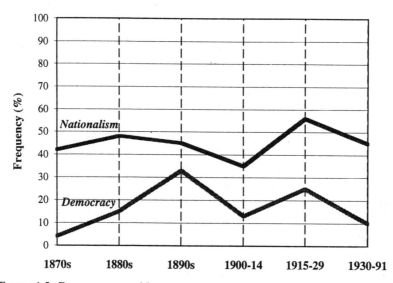

FIGURE 1.5: DEMOCRACY AND NATIONALISM.

Democracy and nationalism are distinct but closely related themes. As this graph suggests, sentiments of nationalism—both pro-America and antiforeign—appear more frequently in Yellowstone accounts than do sentiments of pride in the democratic nature of American politics. However, nationalistic statements and comparisons can be interpreted as descriptive vehicles—the jargon of nineteenth-century nature writing—rather than as expressing genuine, nationalistic feelings.

At the time of Yellowstone's establishment, Americans were creating a new mythology for themselves and their young nation. A combination of religion, nationalism, and the idea of nature as sublime permeated popular literature and gave it "a special descriptive power that lay at the heart of the new mythology."[51] The American public wanted to believe in the fledgling nation's divinely ordained success, and Yellowstone's discovery and establishment as a national park went hand in hand with such beliefs. John Stoddard's description of Yellowstone typifies this mind-set:

> On three sides this is guarded by lofty, well-nigh inaccessible mountains, as though the Infinite Himself would not allow mankind to rashly enter its sublime enclosure. In this respect our Government has wisely imitated the Creator. It has proclaimed to all the world the sanctity of this peculiar area. It has received it as a gift from God and, as His trustee, holds it for the welfare of humanity.[52]

Some park scholars have gone so far as to assert that a strong nationalistic sentiment was the most important impetus behind Yellowstone's establishment. "For decades," Runte writes, "the nation had suffered the embarrassment of a dearth of recognized cultural achievements" and the spectacular scenery of the West was heralded as proof of cultural greatness.[53] Again, such observations and conclusions are well founded. The literature describing Yellowstone and other spectacular, natural landscapes of the American West has a distinct, nationalistic tone and is full of "See-America-First" slogans. However, it is hard to separate purely nationalistic intentions from the literary tradition of the times. Religion and appreciation for the sublime are mentioned as often as—and usually in conjunction with—nationalism as the purpose(s) for establishing national parks, yet the role of religion is ignored in most arguments supporting the singular importance of nationalism.

Indeed, evidence of nationalism can be found in the use of Gothic architectural terms to compare the shapes of geologic features in the national parks to European castles and cathedrals. Comparisons to Europe are abundant throughout the Yellowstone literature. However, they are not solely nationalistic in tone as in this description of Yellowstone's Grand Canyon:

> Gothic arches, Corinthian capitals and Egyptian basilicas built before human architecture was born . . . Gibraltars and Sebastopols that never can be taken; Alhambras, where kings of strength and queens of beauty reigned long before the first earthly crown was empearled . . . a new and divinely inspired revelation, the Old Testament written on papyrus, the New Testament written on parchment, and now this Last Testament written on the rocks.[54]

Repeatedly in the Yellowstone literature, the size, shape, beauty, and antiquity of America's natural landscapes were compared to both natural and built features of Europe, particularly the Alps and Gothic architectural structures. One magazine editor even capitalized on the use of superlatives and patriotic language in Yellowstone descriptions to poke fun at the use of European comparisons:

> Why should we waste ourselves in unpatriotic wonderment over the gorge of the Tamina or the Via Mala, when nature has furnished us with the Grand Cañon of the Yellowstone, in which the famed Swiss ravines would be but as a crevice or a wrinkle? Why run across the sea to stifle and sneeze

over the ill odors of Solfaterra, when we can spoil our lungs or our trousers to better effect, and on an incomparably larger scale, with the gigantic boiling springs and geysers of Montana?[55]

In the Yellowstone record, comparisons to the eastern United States and other American national parks are at least as common as are comparisons to Europe (figure 1.6). And, although Yellowstone's geysers and hot springs were constantly compared to those of Iceland and New Zealand—as they were in the discovery accounts—the elevation of Yellowstone Lake is constantly compared to the height of New Hampshire's Mt. Washington: a tradition started in 1870 by Gustavus Doane but passed down through a variety of guidebooks and later publications. The Yellowstone Lake-Mt. Washington comparison can be found in many Yellowstone accounts:

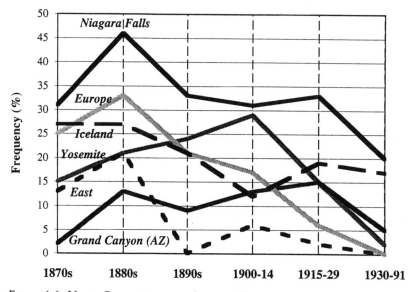

FIGURE 1.6: USE OF COMPARISONS AS A LITERARY DEVICE.
In attempting to describe the Yellowstone region and its individual natural features, authors often compare Yellowstone to more familiar places. Most common is the comparison between Yellowstone's Lower Falls and Niagara Falls. Comparisons to Europe—especially the Alps—peak in the 1880s and then fall off rapidly, being surpassed by comparisons to Yosemite National Park and the Grand Canyon in Arizona. Comparing Yellowstone's thermal areas to those of Iceland (and New Zealand) has been consistently popular throughout the park's history.

The one point which surprised us all was the remarkable altitude of this large sheet of water—7,788 feet above the sea. If our own Mount Washington, of which we New Englanders are all so justly proud, should by some accident be dropped down in the Yellowstone Lake, we should never be able to recover him; for his base should go down to the sea-level, his topmost stone would then be one half a mile below the surface of the water.[56]

Other comparisons were typically made between Yellowstone's Lower Falls and Niagara Falls. And comparisons between Yellowstone's mountains and those of Europe—especially the Alps—peak in the 1880s and then fall off rapidly, being surpassed by comparisons to Yosemite Park and the Grand Canyon in Arizona.

The owners of westward-expanding railroads and some politicians certainly had ulterior motives for using nationalistic language in promoting the establishment of national parks, but for most park visitors, these comparisons to Europe were more likely descriptive vehicles rather than forms of nationalism. European comparisons were used because these were familiar terms in common use and presented the best means of communicating the dimensions and impact of the landscape.

As in the wilderness theme, democracy is often used to voice approval and recognition of the federal government's commitment to protect and preserve Yellowstone for all people. After viewing an eruption of Castle Geyser, one prominent traveler, lecturer, and essayist wrote: "I realized then, as never before the noble action of our Government in giving this incomparable region to the people . . . thanks to the generosity of Congress, the Park itself, and everything that it contains, are absolutely free to all, rich and poor, native and foreigner,—forever consecrated to the education and delight of man."[57] Such comments are not nationalistic so much as they are indicative of pride in a democratic system.

The idea of the democratic nature of the park finds one of its strongest expressions in the democratic mix of Yellowstone tourists. Park literature is full of comments describing the variety of people who come to the park:

> The jolly tourists who hail from every corner of the globe . . . are all imbued with the happy-go-lucky, get-there-quick American spirit. Among them we find a Chinese doctor, an African missionary, a Spanish opera star, several titled Englishmen, merry school teachers bound for a joyous holiday away from the crowded schoolrooms; lawyers who seek diversion from the humdrums of the courts . . . all making up a happy band of pilgrims, bound for the wonderland of the Yellowstone.[58]

Park tourists are characterized not only by their diverse nationalities, backgrounds, and reasons for travel, but by their varied social and economic statuses as well. In the park, "a man's dress gave no clue to his vocation or social position. The wearer of a dilapidated hat, ancient blouse and trowsers showing signs of frequent acquaintance with the saddle, was a U.S. Engineer officer in charge of a construction party. His far better clothed companion was one of his teamsters."[59]

Signs of an appreciation for the democratic nature of park tourists is visible even today as a ranger describes the temporary residents of a Yellowstone campground on a typical summer evening: "Next to the forty-thousand-dollar mobile home laden with dignified retirees is a literal commune of one- or two-person tents, suffused in a light haze of illegal smoke and heavy music. Next to the Mormons, the Episcopalians; the Democrats, the Birchers; the gun nuts, the bleeding hearts. It's not a melting pot, but it's a hell of a mixing bowl."[60] As a uniquely American institution—as a park for the masses—Yellowstone National Park is a recognized success:

> In the flush of the moment, I began to think of this park as the repository of things American. It is a place where we can be free: free from the telephone, free to climb a mountain, free from structure, free to fish, free from urban noise, free to cook on a campfire, free from the clock, free to do nothing. . . . I couldn't help think, as I drove home to my cabin, that freedom runs as a thread in this park.[61]

Education: "For the benefit and instruction of the people"

At first glance, education seems less complex a theme than many aforementioned ones. However, people have interpreted Yellowstone's meaning as a place to learn in a variety of ways. An educational trip to Yellowstone can be seen as "the ideal summer school of nature study" as well as a place to learn moral and civic lessons.[62] For John Muir, a strong voice for the value of an outdoor education, the national parks were "universities without walls." In Yellowstone, Muir encouraged people to "take a look into a few of the tertiary volumes of the grand geological library of the park, and see how God writes history. No technical knowledge is required; only a calm day and a calm mind . . . a wonderful set of volumes lying on their sides,—books a million years old, well bound, miles in size, with full page illustrations."[63]

Accounts of travel to the park indicate that people continue to view the

Yellowstone experience as an educational one. People still come to Yellowstone eager to learn. A former interpretive ranger reports, "Many people come to us already fired up about the park, and we get to deal with them when they are most receptive to new ideas, most willing to be taught."[64] However, the park's literary record indicates that today there is less individually motivated learning and more reliance on being taught by others. Many tourists wishing to learn about the park participate in organized activities: joining ranger-led nature walks and talks, watching educational films in the visitor centers, examining museum displays, or taking part in summer field schools taught in the park.

Education is not mentioned as frequently as other elements of a Yellowstone experience, although its counterpart—the use of the park for science and scientific investigation—figures quite prominently during at least the park's first few decades (figure 1.7).

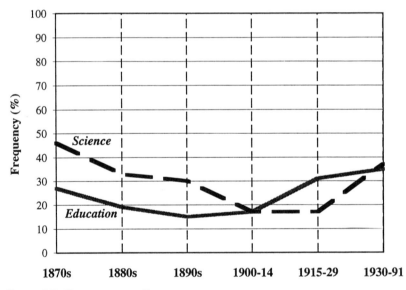

FIGURE 1.7: EDUCATION AND SCIENCE.
In the park's early decades, it is easier to distinguish between the two themes, but there is a blurring of boundaries and definitions by the latter half of the twentieth century. In the park's first decades, the education provided by a Yellowstone experience was not as scientific as it is considered to be today. Instead, a Yellowstone experience provided an education in moral, civic, and religious principles as well as the principles of science. Both themes are found in lower frequencies in the literature than are many other themes, but they are evident throughout the park's history.

Already at the time of the park's discovery, the park's value to science was noted: "I returned to camp in the evening profoundly impressed with the greatness of the phenomena we were witnessing from day to day, and of their probable future importance to science, in unraveling mysteries hitherto unsolvable."[65] The very creation of the park was heralded as "a tribute from our legislators to science, and the gratitude of the nation of men of science in all parts of the world is due them for this munificent donation."[66]

One educational activity that has become an institution within the national parks is the campfire program. Sitting around a campfire while a ranger interprets the park is a wonderful blend of many of the park's traditions. It combines an element of wilderness recreation with an aura of the Wild West, the camaraderie of democratic tourism, and a chance to learn about the park:

> I feel about campfire programs the same way I feel about rangers. Whatever happens to the parks, whatever political ills befall them, this faltering institution—the old campfire circle—simply must go on. Even when bloated and electronically sterilized, it is one of the unexpected blessings of a visit to Yellowstone, a touch of what's best about sharing the woods. Philosophers emphasize the solitariness of wilderness experience, and I approve; the renewal and stimulation to be had alone with nature is priceless. But national parks are more than wilderness. They are outposts on the edges, from which people can go, or at least peer, in. And the outposts, be they campgrounds, museums, or even hotels, can be enriching. . . . And, if the ranger is any good at his work, if the fire crackles and crumbles hospitably as they sit, and if the smoke that stings their eyes that night surprises them a few days later when they next put that coat on, their Yellowstone campfire will never go out.[67]

In the 125 years since Yellowstone's establishment, the world, the United States, the National Park Service, and Yellowstone itself have undergone many changes, some more disruptive and unsettling than others. In this atmosphere of change, however, an image of Yellowstone as a unique place has persisted, and this image is one of tradition. All of the themes mentioned above—an appreciation for the park's beauty, its uniqueness, its tourism and recreation capabilities, its wildness, democratic ownership, and educational qualities have persisted over time. Yellowstone's evolution has not been one of haphazard change, nor can it be directly correlated to swings in national opinion on how to manage nature and nature preserves. An examination of Yellowstone's record shows that despite minor changes in the overall popularity of certain elements of the park experience, some basic themes within the park experience have endured since the park's creation. This permanence is rarely if ever addressed by park scholars, possibly because history is typically thought of in terms of change. But history and evolution are not only characterized by change, and it is in the long periods of little change—those periods of quiet concern, admiration, and enjoyment of the park—that Yellowstone's spirit of place evolved.

2

DISCOVERY ACCOUNTS

Over the past century, much time and effort has been spent search-
ing for origins, beginnings, or "firsts" in Yellowstone. Yellowstone's
physical landscape has been combed for evidence of the park's first human
inhabitants and Anglo-European visitors.[1] Even the origins of such concep-
tual things as place-names and road systems have been studied and catego-
rized.[2] Recent scholarship indicates that Native Americans were the first to
recognize a spirit of place unique to the Yellowstone region centuries before
whites entered the surrounding areas.[3] For those interested in the national
parks, especially, Yellowstone is important as the place where the national
park idea supposedly originated. And, like the park's physical landscape, its
literary landscape has been laboriously dissected and scrutinized in the hopes
of finding evidence documenting the circumstances surrounding the park's
creation.[4] However, in their search for heroes and sacred places, these archae-
ologists of the park's written record have failed to recognize that Yellowstone's
importance to us lies not only in its designation as a national park but, perhaps more importantly, in its qualities as place.

Yellowstone's origin as place is distinct from its origin as a national park.
The latter can be pinpointed in time: 1 March 1872. Yellowstone's origin as
place, however, is less exact. It began with the publication of the "discovery"
accounts—the first widely read accounts describing the region that would
become Yellowstone National Park—and continued to evolve or unfold over
several decades. Those who provided the public with its first vicarious views
of Yellowstone played a disproportionately large role in determining the cultural evolution of the park, because the language those discoverers chose to
describe the region's physical and affective qualities—the specific words, met-
aphors, and meanings they attached to the region—provided the seeds from
which the park's sense of place grew.

"DISCOVERERS" AND "DISCOVERY" ACCOUNTS

Rarely are those who first encounter terra incognita honored as its official discoverers. Instead, the title "discoverer" is typically bestowed on those who first communicate new geographic information to others. It is through language—speech, literature, and artistic endeavors—that people make places visible and real, creating places where none existed.[5] Such was the case in Yellowstone. The members of three exploratory expeditions are typically credited with discovering the region that became Yellowstone National Park: the Folsom-Cook-Peterson expedition of 1869, the Washburn-Langford-Doane expedition of 1870, and the Hayden Survey of 1871.[6]

But these men were certainly not the first to see Yellowstone. Generations of Native Americans and scores of fur trappers and miners preceded these "discoverers" into the upper reaches of the Yellowstone River. Nevertheless, members of the Folsom, Washburn, and Hayden expeditions are considered by national park scholars to be the park's official discoverers. With their words as much as with their deeds, these explorers "discovered" Yellowstone for the American public and "made particular and important contributions to the emerging popular image of the Yellowstone wonderland."[7] Hence, the park's official discoverers were not the first to see the Yellowstone region but were the first to communicate on a national scale the region's existence, location, and physical characteristics. As a result, Yellowstone's debut on the national consciousness occurred when word of its existence appeared in the articles written by the members of these expeditions.

David E. Folsom, Charles W. Cook, and William Peterson, would-be prospectors and, at the time, fellow ditchdiggers in Helena, Montana Territory, set out on an admittedly impetuous journey into the Yellowstone country in the summer of 1869. Their attempts to publicize their adventures and the sights seen during their travels, however, met with little early success. The editors at two periodicals rejected an account written by Cook and Folsom, stating they would not risk their reputations on "such unreliable material."[8] A more sympathetic editor was finally found at the *Western Monthly Magazine* in Chicago.

The following year, spurred on by the fantastic stories of the previous year's expedition, General Henry D. Washburn, Nathaniel P. Langford, and Lieutenant Gustavus C. Doane of the Second Cavalry led a party of nineteen into Yellowstone. Among their number was Truman Everts, a man who had the misfortune of being separated from his comrades and who wandered lost in the interior of what would become the park for thirty-seven days until he was finally rescued by a local trapper. His misadventure led to a thrilling and none-too-modest narrative of his ordeal.[9] The Washburn party's return resulted in a flurry of newspaper and magazine articles, most of which appeared first in local papers but spread quickly to the national press. Langford sent his account of the expedition to *Scribner's Monthly*, which assured him and his portrayal of the expedition an immediate and national audience. Langford also toured the country giving lectures about the newly discovered region. His lecture circuit was sponsored by Jay Cooke of the Northern Pacific Railroad along whose lines the soon-to-be-established park would lie.

After hearing and reading about the Yellowstone region, Professor Ferdinand V. Hayden of the United States Geological and Geographical Survey of the Territories promptly requested funds from Congress to undertake his own, official, government-sponsored expedition. He headed west the following year and was lucky enough to have several illustrators in his entourage, two of whom owe the success of their careers to their involvement with the Hayden expedition of 1871. Thomas Moran, who had drawn sketches for Langford's articles published in *Scribner's* the previous year, was one. Moran was eager to see Yellowstone for himself. The other artist was William Henry Jackson, a young but very capable photographer.

Although the park's discoverers wrote or collaborated on a variety of other articles, which were published separately at later dates, the "discovery accounts" referred to here consist of a number of articles and government documents written by members of the 1869, 1870, and 1871 expeditions. These include: Charles Cook and David E. Folsom's "The Valley of the Upper Yellowstone" in the *Western Monthly Magazine* of July 1870; Henry D. Washburn's "The Yellowstone Expedition" in the *Helena Daily Herald* of September 1870 and the *New York Times* and the *Pioneer Press* (St. Paul, Minnesota) of October 1870; Nathaniel P. Langford's "The Wonders of the Yellowstone," parts 1 and 2, in *Scribner's Monthly* of May and June 1871, respectively; Walter Trumbull's "The Washburn Yellowstone Expedition," numbers 1 and 2, in *Overland Monthly* of May and June 1871, respectively; Truman Everts's "Thirty-Seven Days of Peril" in *Scribner's Monthly* of November 1871; Gustavus Doane's Senate Executive Document Number 51, 41st Congressional Session of 1871; and Ferdinand V. Hayden's *Preliminary Report of the United States Geological Survey of Montana and Portions of Adjacent Territories* of 1872.[10]

An eighth account written by Captains John W. Barlow and David P. Heap of the Corps of Engineers might be added to the list of discovery accounts, although its authors are typically not included on any lists of "official discoverers." In the summer and fall of 1871, simultaneous with the 1871 Hayden expedition, Barlow and Heap led a similar expedition into the Yellowstone region. Published after Hayden's report and with less fanfare, the Barlow-Heap report provided detailed information about the park, much of which was later used by guidebook and other authors. As fate would have it, however, the great Chicago fire of 1871 destroyed the Barlow-Heap expedition's photographs and scientific reports. Hence, due purely to the chance event of the Chicago fire, the data, specimens, sketches, and photographs collected by the Hayden expedition became all the more important as the first—and at that time, only—source of reliable, scientific information about Yellowstone.

Rather than offering the public seven different views of the newly explored Yellowstone region, the discovery accounts were amazingly alike. If, as others have shown, explorers are "preprogrammed" to respond to the regions they explore in particular ways, Yellowstone's explorers were no exception.[11] Four factors acting separately and in concert helped focus the discoverers' attention on certain aspects of the Yellowstone landscape and narrowed their interpretation and description of it. First, the park's discoverers all had knowledge of "prediscovery" accounts describing Yellowstone. Second, the discoverers set out for the upper reaches of the Yellowstone River at a time of worldwide scientific and geographic exploration. Having read of other expeditions in distant lands, they were aware of their own participation in and contribution to a growing body of exploration literature. Third, Yellowstone's discoverers were greatly influenced by each other. And finally, the discoverers all wrote in the language of their day, obeying linguistic convention and couching their descriptions in familiar terms. Such a writing style made their reports believable, acceptable, and popular with their intended audiences.

PREDISCOVERY ACCOUNTS

As mentioned earlier, the real discovery of the area that became Yellowstone National Park predates its official discovery. More than a handful of accounts describing parts of the Yellowstone landscape, most notably its thermal features, Yellowstone Lake, and the Grand Canyon, were published well before the first of the official discovery expeditions were organized, and many date back to the fur trade era of the 1820s.[12] However, such prediscovery accounts reached only a limited audience and most were considered "tall tales." In local towns and mining camps, rumors had circulated for years about the strange sights, smells, and sounds of the Upper Yellowstone Valley. The inaccessibility of the Yellowstone plateau, however, kept the region secret from a more national public who knew little or nothing about the region until reading reports of its official discovery.

By the 1860s, only bits and pieces of the vast, geographical knowledge accumulated by Rocky Mountain fur trappers and prospectors had found its way into print, although trappers and miners had unquestionably visited Yellowstone prior to its official discovery. In their accounts, members of all three discovery expeditions described Yellowstone as a terra incognita, yet they repeatedly mentioned finding signs of previous occupation. Members of the Washburn expedition noted in their diaries and published articles that they were probably the first white men ever to view Yellowstone Lake, touting the lake as secluded and pristine and their reaching it a heroic achievement. In almost the same breath, however, these same men told of finding a well-built hunting blind or "rifle-pit" along the lakeshore.[13] In other parts of the park, they reported finding prospect holes and blazed trees, evidence that miners had preceded them. Hayden's *Preliminary Report* of 1872 is full of comments that would lead his readers to believe that Yellowstone was anything but an unknown, uncharted land. In different instances, Hayden wrote, "We followed a well-worn path," or "We were informed by mountain-men that these earthquake shocks are not uncommon," and "The impression among the mountain-men was, that this . . . periodic spring . . . played once in six hours precisely."[14]

More interesting than their comments of finding physical evidence of earlier visitation is the specific language used by the discoverers to describe park features. The particular words, analogies, and phrases chosen by the discoverers to relate their adventures and experiences suggest that previously written documents were both available to and deemed credible by the park's discoverers. In writing their own reports, the discoverers borrowed freely from prediscovery accounts written by fur trappers and prospectors. One such trapper was Joe Meek who hunted in the Yellowstone region in the 1830s. In a biography published the year before Hayden led his survey team into the Upper Yellowstone Valley, the trapper was quoted comparing one of Yellowstone's geyser basins to "the City of Pittsburg."[15] In his official report, Hayden described his initial reaction to the geyser basins with, "I can compare the view to nothing but that of some manufacturing city like Pittsburgh."[16]

Frances Fuller Victor, Joe Meek's biographer, discounted the importance of the earliest rumors and stories of the Yellowstone region. She stated: "The important fact to remember is that this knowledge was barren of result. For the most part it existed only in the minds of illiterate men and perished with them. It never caught the public ear and did not in the least degree hasten the final discovery."[17] Yet, a later Yellowstone historian suggested that "the cumulative effect of such reports and rumors, however, was destined soon to convince intelligent listeners that no wild tale could be so persistent, and there must be something at the headwaters of the Yellowstone worth looking into."[18]

Regardless of whether foreknowledge of Yellowstone's existence spurred its eventual discovery, the fact remains that the discoverers were affected by what they had read prior to their actual arrival in Yellowstone. They came to the park not only with expectations of what they would find but with a well-worn vocabulary with which to communicate their findings to the world.

LANGUAGE OF EXPLORATION

The eighteenth and nineteenth centuries were times of great explorations. From the poles to the abyssal depths of the sea, explorers embarked on religious as well as scientific quests hoping to find evidence of God's plan and purpose for the earth. A belief in natural theology and the sublime in nature colored the lenses through which explorers viewed their discoveries, just as it affected the language of nature writing and the dimensions of landscape art during this age. Members of the Folsom expedition excepted, Yellowstone's discoverers most likely prepared themselves for their journey into Yellowstone's unknown by reading the works of their contemporaries who were actively exploring other parts of the globe. And, they incorporated the language of other discoverers and discoveries into their descriptions of Yellowstone.

One important source for both Langford and Hayden was the 1863 work of Dr. Ferdinand Hochstetter on the thermal areas of New Zealand. A decade earlier, Hochstetter had referred to the hot springs at Rotomahana as luxurious bathing pools of "purest marble" with "crystal-clear water."[19] Hochstetter told of pools in which one could choose a bath temperature by sitting in the warmer pools at the top of the spring or cooler pools further from the source. Continuing, Hochstetter wrote, "Immense clouds of steam, reflecting the beautiful blue of the basin . . . present an aspect which no description or illustration is able to represent. It has the appearance of a cataract plunging over natural shelves, which, as it falls, is suddenly turned to stone."[20] Using similar language, Hayden wrote of the azure blueness of the water in Yellowstone's Mammoth Hot Springs and suggested that they were "bathing-pools . . . arranged one above the other" and "had the appearance of a frozen cascade" or "the appearance of water congealed by frost as it quickly flows down a rocky declivity."[21] Hayden's assistant, A. C. Peale, concurred by stating that "the whole mass looked like some grand cascade that had been suddenly arrested in its descent, and frozen."[22] The following year, Peale repeated his Hochstetterlike description of the Mammoth springs: "The water in all of them is either warm or hot according to their position, the lower ones having the coolest water. The water has also that exquisitely beautiful blue tint which is beyond description, and which forms such handsome contrasts to the white, marble-like basins."[23]

It can be argued that the metaphor of a waterfall may not reflect Hochstetter's influence so much as a valid depiction of reality: the Mammoth Hot Springs terraces *do* look like frozen waterfalls. Also, the waterfall is a strong and pervasive symbol in the language of the sublime and may have come to mind for that reason as well. However, it cannot be denied that Hayden and Peale's prior reading of Hochstetter's *Neu = Seeland* affected the way they interpreted and described similar thermal features in Yellowstone. Further, by including excerpts from Hochstetter's work in his report to Congress, Hayden gave credibility to his own interpretation of the Mammoth terraces. To a public relatively ignorant of the nature of hot springs, Hayden's description, corroborated by Hochstetter's similar description of springs in New Zealand, surely must have seemed a true and authoritative depiction of reality.

Nathaniel Langford did not see the Mammoth Hot Springs during his discovery expedition of 1870, so his widely distributed and immensely popular articles in *Scribner's* did not mention the terraces. However, when he finally did see the terraces in 1873, he described them as "congealed cascades, apparently frozen in their descent" and having a whiteness that "exceeds that of purest alabaster."[24] Further evidence of Langford's familiarity with Hochstetter's work appears in his discovery account when Langford wrote enthusiastically about the Yellowstone region: "We can only say that the field is open for exploration—illimitable in resource, grand in extent, wonderful in variety, in a climate favored of Heaven, and amid scenery the most stupendous on the continent."[25] This passage is almost a direct translation of Hochstetter's previously published praise for New Zealand as a tourist attraction.[26] Whether consciously or subconsciously, causally or coincidentally, Langford borrowed from Hochstetter while writing his descriptions of Yellowstone.

Closer to home, the Yellowstone explorers relied heavily upon each other as sources of information, vocabulary, and inspiration. Members of Hayden's expedition, especially, read everything published by the two previous expeditions. Lieutenant Gustavus Doane, leader of the military escort that accompanied the 1870 expedition, published his journal in March of 1871, and Hayden read it in preparation for his own expedition. Hayden praised Doane's work: "For graphic description and thrilling interest, it has not been surpassed by any official report made to our government since the times of Lewis and Clark."[27] The influence of Doane's report on Hayden's subsequent choice of words is obvious. In seeing the bubbling mud pots at Mud Volcano, Doane wrote:

> A Plasterer . . . would go into ecstasies over this mortar, which is worked to such a degree of fineness that it can be dried in large lumps, either in the sun, or in a fire, without a sign of cracking, and when once dry is a soft finely grained stone, resembling clay slate when dark, or meerschaum when white. Mortar might well be good after being constantly worked for perhaps ten thousand years.[28]

The following year, Hayden wrote, "This mud, which has been wrought in these caldrons for perhaps hundreds of years, is so fine and pure that the manufacturer of porcelain-ware would go into ecstasy at the sight. The contents of many of the springs are of such a snowy whiteness that, when dried in cakes in the sun or by a fire, they resemble the finest meerschaum."[29]

It is more difficult, however, to decipher the originator of Doane's descriptions. During most of the 1870 expedition, Doane suffered from a severely infected right thumb, which made keeping his diary up to date an impossibility. By the time the swollen digit was lanced and healing, much of the journey had been completed. In order to catch up on missing journal entries, the lieutenant spent much of his free time copying from Langford's journal into his own. One example of journal copying is found in the similarities in descriptions of Giantess Geyser in eruption. The three expedition leaders—Washburn, Langford, and Doane—shared a common perception of the experience, which is not likely to be due purely to chance. Langford wrote that sunlight on the eruptive spray was like "a luminous circle radiant with all the colors of the prism, and resembling the halo of glory represented in paintings as encircling the head of Divinity."[30] Doane wrote that "rainbows encircle the summits of the jets with a halo of celestial glory."[31] Washburn went into more detail but painted essentially the same picture: "Standing and looking down into the steam and vapor of the crater of the Giantess, with the sun upon your back, the shadow is surrounded by a beautiful rainbow, and by getting the proper angle, the rainbow, surrounding only the head, gives that halo so many painters have vainly tried to give in paintings of the Savior."[32] Since Hayden's 1871 party did not see Giantess in eruption, Hayden included Langford's description of Giantess in his report along with Langford's descriptions of Giant and Beehive Geysers taken directly from the *Scribner's* articles.

Hayden borrowed heavily, too, from the Cook-Folsom discovery account, especially in his descriptions of the thermal features. He relied on Cook and Folsom's terms when he pictured the geyserite formations as "beadwork" and "frostwork" and likened the mud pots to bowls of "mush." In different instances, the mud pots reminded Hayden alternately of thick mush, boiling mush, kettles of mush, and caldrons of mush. The mush analogy, however, can be traced back further than Folsom and Cook to a fur trapper named Daniel Potts who wrote to his family of his travels through the Yellowstone region some fifty years earlier. Potts's letter was published without an author in a Philadelphia newspaper in 1827.

"Like men of every age, we see in Nature what we have been taught to look for, we feel what we have been prepared to feel" and in Yellowstone, the discoverers were prepared to experience the sublime.[33] Even David Folsom, miner and ditchdigger, was well versed in the language of the sublime. In his description of Yellowstone's Grand Canyon published in 1870, Folsom wrote, "We returned to camp realizing, as we have never done before, how utterly insignificant are man's mightiest efforts when compared with the fulfillment of Omnipotent will. Language is entirely inadequate to convey a just conception of the awful grandeur and sublimity of this masterpiece of nature's handiwork."[34] Ferdinand Hayden's writing style proves him to be more than the analytical, unemotional scientist. His *Preliminary Report* of 1872 is a marvelous blend of objective, scientific observation and subjective, descriptive prose strongly influenced by the idea of the sublime. Page after page of all of the discoverers' accounts is filled with elements of the language of the sublime. As described by the discoverers, Yellowstone's almost mythic landscape is beautiful beyond description, the handiwork of God or nature, and far beyond the reach of human artistic endeavors. It inspires religious, intellectual, scientific, patriotic, and artistic contemplation. Yellowstone is dangerous yet fascinating, full of extraordinary and unbelievable features, and all are there for the purpose of amusing, teaching, and inspiring the American public. The idea of nature as sublime and the literary conventions associated with the language of the sublime are the most prevalent characteristics shared by not only the discoverers in their discovery accounts but also by Yellowstone writers for the next half century.

Another example of how popular phrases and literary devices found their way into the Yellowstone record is the appearance and use of the term "freak." However, unlike the language of the sublime, the term "freak of nature" has changed its meaning or flavor over the course of the past century. Typical interpretation of the phrase by park scholars is that Yellowstone's natural wonders were intriguing and of value to the public because such features were oddities or "freaks" of nature. By singling out the term "freak" and placing it in quotation marks, historians would have us believe that Yellowstone was viewed as a modern-day sideshow that aroused a type of curiosity mixed with disgust or fear and distracted tourists from what was really important: the park's natural ecosystems. Interpreted in this way, freak of nature is not a term of endearment.

However, a close examination of Yellowstone's written record—as well as the language used to describe other national parks and newly discovered regions of the American West during the late 1800s—shows that the term "freak" was a popular, vernacular way of describing singularities, not abnormalities. The terms "freak of nature," "freak of the elements," and "freak of Nature's handiwork" are sprinkled liberally throughout the discovery accounts and are used synonymously with "marvel of nature" or "miracle of nature." The frequency with which "freak of nature" appears is probably due in part to its connection with the scientific aspect of the sublime. Elizabeth McKinsey includes in her explanation of the sublime that "part of the quest for facts and statistics was a taste for 'Singularities'—for the unique features of a landscape, for the new and unusual, and therefore, the surprising."[35] Hence, noting nature's "freaks" was deemed scientific and no different or less important than noting nature as beautiful, inspirational, or moralistic. Almon Gunnison, upon setting out for his journey to Yellowstone with three companions, one of whom was a geology professor from Boston, wrote, "The Professor is elated, for we are going towards wonder-land, and he has absorbing passion for freaks of nature and curious forms of rock and stone."[36]

In modern parlance, the word freak denotes something bizarre and intimates a negative response. During the 1800s, the word had a different connotation. A freak was a lighthearted prank or frivolity. "Freak of nature" described the playful, beautiful, unique way in which nature sometimes expressed itself. In the Yellowstone literature, the term "freak" was applied to many different conditions and situations. Langford, in his discovery account, described the incrustations around the hot springs as "the most delicate and wonderful freaks of nature's handiwork."[37] And a tourist wrote that nature had painted the Grand Canyon "in a rapturous freak of her mysterious wonder-working."[38] Yellowstone's Isa Lake, thermal features generally, the Devil's Slide, Fishing Cone, and the Wedded Trees were all referred to as freaks. In contrast, however, the marvelous Old Faithful Inn was considered "not in the least a freaky affair."[39]

One of the most beautiful examples of how people interpreted the idea of freaks is this description of wildflowers in the mountains of Colorado:

We find as many strange freaks in the vegetable kingdom here as elsewhere in the Rocky Mountains. Morning after morning in midsummer have we shaken the thick, crisp scales of white frost from our blankets, and looked sorrowfully around upon a scene of apparent desolation. Brilliant flowers of the evening before were a mass of wilted ruins and the splendid tall bluegrass, that looked a delicious morsel for stock at sunset, was bent and sometimes broken with its weight of a night's winter. But an hour of sunshine always changed the scene to one of springtime freshness, and often the flora seeming the most delicate rallies first under its magic influence.[40]

That tiny flowers could recuperate from what should have been a killing frost truly constituted a freak or unique example of nature's wonders.

The literature of the late 1800s and early 1900s assigned the freak of nature label to many features with no hint that it was meant to discount or reduce affection for the feature. Pikes Peak in Colorado, for example, was described as a place with "peculiar freaks of sculpture and feats of architecture" where even "the clouds were full of freaks that drew forth loud exclamations of wonder and surprise."[41] Yellowstone National Park was indeed set aside because it contained so many marvelous freaks of nature. But to relegate people's feelings for park features to idle curiosity or ogling at a circus sideshow is to do the park a disservice and its patrons a dishonor. The park's literary record should be read and interpreted in the same light in which it was written.

It was a combination of factors that caused the discovery accounts to be more alike than disparate. And, rather than challenging the discoverers' descriptions of Yellowstone with new information and interpretations of the region, subsequent descriptions of the park relied heavily on the information available in the discovery accounts. With few exceptions, authors of Yellowstone articles, books, and guidebooks published in the 1870s and 1880s incorporated the discoverers' descriptions into their own texts. As a result, the words of the discoverers reached an extensive national and international audience and came to cast a broad yet distinct shadow on Yellowstone's evolution as a distinct, nationally recognized place.

PUBLICIZING YELLOWSTONE

Immediately following Yellowstone's establishment as "The National Park," a flurry of magazine articles, guidebooks, tourist brochures, and western narratives were published, most of which consisted primarily of edited versions of the discovery accounts (table 2.1). And, by the turn of the century, popularizing "The Yellowstone" became a respectable career not only for the discoverers but for those who hoped to build their own reputations as scientists, politicians, or businessmen. These Yellowstone "legend-builders" had strong ties to money, the press, and the federal government, and they put these connections to use in promoting the park and themselves.[42] Railroad companies envisioned the economic opportunity of the region and quickly hired writers to "sell" the park and its environs to tourists and settlers by writing guidebooks and manuals.[43] By using familiar terms and the literary conventions of their day, park promoters eased the transmission of information and made the public comfortable with and receptive to their descriptions of the park.

In an effort to be first to publish news of Yellowstone and details of the region's unusual and unique features, authors of early guidebooks tended to merely copy passages from the discovery accounts rather than undertake an expensive, difficult, and often dangerous journey to the distant park to compile material to be used in their accounts. Hence, the image of Yellowstone as perceived and portrayed by the discoverers was rapidly disseminated to a much broader audience than the discovery accounts could reach alone. Sheer repetition strengthened the believability of the discoverers' image by making it appear that most travelers and travel writers were similarly affected by the park landscape.

Many authors of early Yellowstone guidebooks were forced to use the accounts of the discoverers, because they had not yet seen the park for themselves. A minority confessed, apologized, and offered some sort of excuse: "As time did not admit of my visiting these wonders, I present drawings thereof, from original sketches by Mr. Langford's party."[44] Others tried to write as if they had visited the park but betrayed themselves by assigning the wrong names or locations to park features and by copying obviously erroneous information. Robert Strahorn, writer for and employee of the Union Pacific Railroad, told his readers that he found "stone snakes, toads and fishes" along with other petrified items on Yellowstone's Specimen Ridge.[45] Had Strahorn actually climbed Specimen Ridge or been more familiar with his literary sources, he would quickly have realized the absurdity of his transposed stories.

One of the first guidebooks to appear was James Richardson's 1872 edition of *Wonders of the Yellowstone*, which was made up entirely of passages from the discovery accounts, including J. W. Barlow and D. P. Heap's *Report of a Reconnaissance of the Basin of the Upper Yellowstone in 1871*. The book underwent several editions in the United States and was published in London two years later. A few independent authors contributed to the bank of information from which these and other guidebook authors made withdrawals. H. J. Norton, a resident of nearby Virginia City, Montana, and guidebook author himself, was a favorite source, especially for Strahorn and Henry Winser, an employee of the Northern Pacific Railroad who authored or collaborated on several park guidebooks. Rossiter W. Raymond toured the park in 1871 and wrote of his experiences in a little book entitled *Camp and Cabin*, and Reverend Edwin Stanley, who published *Rambles in Wonderland* about his travels with wife and daughter in the park in 1873, also added greatly to the information available to guidebook authors and editors. By the early 1880s, two other ministers, Reverend Hoyt and Reverend Talmage, were quoted and cited often in Yellowstone books, articles, and travel pamphlets, possibly because it was assumed that their clerical titles gave them—and their impressions of the park—credulity. But, these two men borrowed heavily from the discovery accounts and used the discoverers' reports as a starting point for their descriptions of the park. Hence, with the exception of Norton's guidebook, much of the material in the early guidebooks came from the discovery accounts.

TABLE 2.1: GUIDEBOOKS OF THE LATE 1800S.

Author, Title, and Copyright Date	Remarks
James Richardson, 1872, *Wonders of the Yellowstone*	Originally published in the United States, *Wonders* was published in London in 1874. The author had never been to the park and wrote the book completely from passages taken from accounts by Doane, Langford, Hayden, and Barlow-Heap.
William Cullen Bryant, 1872, *Picturesque America*	An oversized, highly illustrated book, published in parts, about various scenic locations in the United States and edited by Bryant. The chapter on Yellowstone was entitled "Our National Park" and was made up entirely of excerpts from the Hayden and Barlow-Heap reports with illustrations adapted from works by Moran, Jackson, and Holmes.
Harry J. Norton, 1873, *Wonderland Illustrated*	The first real "guidebook" of the park written by an experienced, local author. Some passages were copied from Hayden, but there was much original material.
The Earl of Dunraven, 1876, *The Great Divide*	The book was centered about the earl's 1874 hunting trip to the United States, during which he spent some time in Yellowstone. Much of the text is taken from Hayden's 1872 and 1873 reports as are the illustrations. *The Great Divide* was probably not all that popular in the United States but was widely read in Europe and influenced the writings of subsequent British and continental tourists.
Edwin J. Stanley, 1878, *Rambles in Wonderland*	Rev. Stanley, a native of the Montana Territory, published a book of his travels through the park "for the benefit of friends in the States" after publishing bits and pieces of it in local newspapers. He acknowledged the help of Hayden's and Langford's accounts in completing his work—and these discoverers figured prominently in his text—but much of the book was original in composition.
Robert E. Strahorn, 1879, *To the Rockies and Beyond*	This book promoted settlement along the route of the Union Pacific Railroad and included a chapter on touring Yellowstone Park based on information from secondary sources including the discovery accounts, Norton, and Stanley. Strahorn had not yet visited the park at the time he wrote this particular book, but he wrote it as if he had. Hence, the book was full of inconsistencies and incorrect information.

Robert E. Strahorn, 1881,
The Enchanted Land

In this narrative of his travels in Yellowstone during the fall of 1880, Strahorn included much of the material from his 1879 book but with corrections. Included was a map of the park showing a line of the Union Pacific Railroad servicing the park's interior despite the fact that no railroad lines were ever built into the park.

L. P. Brockett, 1881,
Our Western Empire

Written for the Union Pacific Railroad, Brockett's book covered the American West generally with a chapter on Yellowstone. Brockett probably did not travel to Yellowstone himself but quoted many "eye witnesses" in his narrative and got many facts about the park as well as travel sequences wrong. The author copied much from the previous years' writings of Strahorn who copied from the discovery accounts and earlier guidebooks.

W.W. Wylie, 1882,
Yellowstone National Park

Wylie wrote a guidebook to be used by tourists "going the Wylie Way" and staying at his tent camps rather than hiring guides of their own and staying in the more expensive hotels. His guidebook was compiled from much original material as well as parts of the discovery accounts, earlier guidebooks, and other previously published books. His illustrations were refreshingly new, taken from photographs by H. B. Colfee, rather than copies of works by Moran, Jackson, and Holmes. Wylie was copied extensively by Haupt.

Herman Haupt, 1883,
The Yellowstone National Park

This book was dedicated to the Northern Pacific Railroad and referred readers to Wylie's 1882 guidebook throughout its pages. Haupt quoteds the reports of Yellowstone superintendent Norris as well as various discovery accounts, especially those of Hayden.

Henry J. Winser, 1883,
The Yellowstone National Park: A Manual for Tourists

Winser, affiliated with the Northern Pacific Railroad was one of the first to illustrate a text with sketches taken from F. J. Haynes's photographs. Much of Winser's text was original although he copied from a variety of sources: the discovery accounts, Superintendent Norris's reports, and Rossiter Raymond, among others. Winser was later copied in part by both Campbell and Guptill/Haynes in their series of guidebooks.

John Hyde, 1886,
Official Guide to Yellowstone National Park

Hyde's guidebook was an updated version of Winser's guidebook and was again published in 1890 with W. Riley as author.

Because the distance between Yellowstone Park and most of the country's population centers was considerable, would-be tourists made the decision to visit the park well in advance of their actual journeys. In addition to distance, the expense of the trip coupled with the park's reputation as potentially dangerous prompted tourists to familiarize themselves with the region before leaving home. They prepared themselves mentally as well as physically, and procuring and perusing guidebooks became part of that process. Guidebooks were popular, helpful, often necessary travel aides. People traveling to the park not only used guidebooks but also assumed the information contained therein to be true, kept them handy as references during their park tours, and often committed much of their contents to memory. Statements such as the following are found throughout the park's published accounts: "The tourist after having metaphorically swallowed half a dozen railroad pamphlets and guides between St. Paul and Livingston, and digested as many descriptions of the Yellowstone National Park . . . should see it as others have described it. He should have all the vocabulary in the front row."[46]

Some tourists, unsure of what they would find within the park's boundaries, hired private guides once they reached the outskirts of the park. One guidebook, hoping to appeal to everyone, went so far as to tout its virtues not only as an ersatz to the expense of a personal guide but to an actual visit to the park. The author insisted that "tourists who use this Book will find it unnecessary to employ Guides. Those who cannot visit the Park will find the Book an excellent substitute."[47] Faith in the veracity and competency of the guidebooks is illustrated in a comment a young tourist made in a letter home to her mother. She wrote, "I can tell you what I have done but I can't describe the things I have seen. I believe I will send you a guide book."[48]

Not all visitors were taken in by their guidebooks' often colorful and persuasive language. In 1883, Margaret Cruikshank, a well-seasoned traveler, made this note in her letters: "In my guidebook, I read that the little pools around [Old] Faithful have pink and yellow margins and being constantly wet the colors are 'beautiful beyond description.' Then all I can say is that I must be colorblind. . . . I saw none of these."[49] Nor did Ms. Cruikshank believe the distances between park features or the fine quality of the park roads as advertised in her guidebook: "The miles given are, I believe, surveyors' measures, but never were miles so absurdly understated. Be sure of this, that a Park mile according to the book, is worth any two, if not five, elsewhere. . . . Our man, Isaac Door, an experienced Utah state driver said, 'it was a good fifty miles as he ever drove.' Yet the book called it only thirty-six."[50] Other tourists found fault with their guidebooks, also. In the following, criticism was aimed at H. J. Winser's manual for tourists: "From here onward we rode over a succession of fir clad terraces, 'the charms of which (as the Guide Book says) are apt to cloy.' We found them extremely monotonous, particularly upon a hot day."[51] The passage most likely referred to is from Winser's guidebook wherein he stated, "After leaving the falls and the foaming river, the road soon crosses Cañon Creek, passing for the next eight miles over a succession of pine and fir clad terraces, the charms of which are apt to cloy, before the next attractive point is reached."[52]

Rather than undermining the importance of guidebooks in affecting people's expectations of the park experience, these criticisms emphasize their importance. Guidebooks told people what they should see and do, and visitors followed these instructions obediently. "The local guide-books . . . are filled with enticing pictures of existing splendors; and one humbly visits whatever is set down as necessary to be seen," admitted one tourist.[53] Hence, the repeated behavior of seeing certain sights, participating in certain activities, and experiencing certain emotions eventually manifested the discoverers' image of the Yellowstone experience as reality in the hearts and minds of the public. "Doing" the Yellowstone quickly became an accepted and standardized tradition: "The horses were sent out to a grassy park a mile up the river, to feast upon the nutritious bunch-grass; and as wood was convenient, and hot and cold water in abundance, we were prepared to 'do' the wonders of Wonderland at our leisure."[54]

Over time, recording the criteria of a typical park visit became as important as the trip itself, and a distinct pattern emerges in the park's literary record as people faithfully and consistently document their experiences. Naturally, not all tourists had the money, time, or stamina to "do" the park as thoroughly as others. When this was the case, a sort of disclaimer typically appeared in the account followed by an excerpt from a guidebook or other source:

> We could not give time (two days or more) to travel fifty miles farther in order to see the grandest scene of all in this park of wonders—the Grand Cañon. I am told by everyone who has seen it that it is quite impossible by words or paint-brush to give any idea of its grandeur. As, however, any description of the Park which omits the GRAND CAÑON would be like omitting Hamlet from the play, I will give you this quotation from Professor F. V. Hayden's report to Congress.[55]

Other evidence for the pervasive influence of the guidebooks in promulgating Yellowstone traditions lies in the fact that individuals writing about their own experiences in the park repeated the mistakes printed in their guidebooks. There is dogged repetition in Yellowstone accounts of what had to be understood by at least some as misinformation. Tourists, it seems, would include information in their accounts that seemed unlikely—even preposterous—rather than admit having missed part of the park experience. Evidence of such is found in the persistence of an error in Gustavus Doane's discovery account wherein he described a climb down into Yellowstone's Grand Canyon. In his discovery account, Doane remarked upon the steepness of the canyon walls and the incredible depth of the canyon. Once having reached the river, he noted: "Looking upward the fearful wall appeared to reach the sky. It was about 3 o'clock p.m., and stars could be distinctly seen; so much of the sunlight was cut off from entering the chasm."[56]

John Richardson included Doane's description of this impossible observation in his 1872 guidebook. The same phenomenon was apparently experienced by General Strong—with only a modicum of restraint—during his 1875 visit to the park. The general noticed that "the vertical walls [of the canyon] are seamed and scarred very strangely, and half-way down they narrow up so that the sunlight is almost excluded."[57] Then, in 1887, in his privately published book of travel in the Yellowstone, Theodore Gerrish, too, experienced the midday darkness: "Should you descend and follow the stream in its tortuous course, you would find many places where the overhanging cliffs seem almost to touch each other two thousand feet above your head; and as you peer up between these rocks, you can see stars in the sky each hour in the day."[58]

In interpreting the evolution of Yellowstone's spirit of place, it is important to recognize both the extent to which bits of early accounts were copied into later accounts and the real impetus or intent behind such copying efforts. For example, in *National Parks: The American Experience*, Alfred Runte suggests that the early national parks—Yellowstone and Yosemite in particular— were not necessarily preserved and protected because of people's affection for the places or for environmental/ecological concerns; rather it was because these lands were economically useless for purposes such as agriculture and livestock. From a political standpoint, his point is valid and carries much weight. In Yellowstone's case, congressional and other political documents record a strong effort on the part of those wanting to establish Yellowstone as a national park to convince opponents that the region was worthless. Representative Mark H. Dunnell from the Committee on Public Lands, a leader in the crusade to pass the park bill, presented the following speech to his fellow congressmen:

> The entire area comprised within the limits of the reservation contemplated in this bill, is not susceptible of cultivation with any degree of certainty, and the winters would be too severe for stock-raising. . . . The mountains are all of volcanic origin, and it is not probable that any mines or minerals of value will ever be found there. . . . There is frost every month of the year.
>
> The withdrawal of this tract, therefore, from sale or settlement takes nothing from the value of the public domain, and is no pecuniary loss to the government, but will be regarded by the entire civilized world as a step of progress and an honor to Congress and the nation.[59]

Dunnell, who had not visited the soon-to-be-established national park himself and was not an expert on stock raising, farming, or mining, got his information from Ferdinand Hayden directly and from Hayden's discovery account. Dunnell's—read Hayden's—arguments were then repeated, usually verbatim, by Representative Henry M. Dawes (Massachusetts) and Senators Samuel C. Pomeroy (Kansas) and George F. Edmunds (Vermont) in the House and Senate floor debates. By the time the National Park Act was passed, the worthless lands passage had found its way into most of the National Park Act documents.

But, the "worthless lands" argument was a political construct created to rally support for the Yellowstone bill. It was not the general public's attitude toward the park nor was it the public's justification for removing the Yellowstone region from settlement and occupancy. Many early Yellowstone guidebooks included Dunnell's report to the House pro forma just as they included in their pages a copy of the park's enabling act, a list of elevations, average monthly temperatures, and rules and regulations. Hence, people became familiar with the wording of the Dunnell letter just as they became familiar with the discoverers' impressions of park features. The idea of the park as worthless for any purpose other than tourism appears in the historical record *not* necessarily because it is an idea spontaneously generated in the minds of many different people, but because it is a typical inclusion—one of many— which appeared in many park descriptions of the time.

The public did not need to be convinced of the park's worthlessness to enjoy and appreciate it. One tourist, obviously reciting what he had read, but adding his own observation, wrote, "The Park is of volcanic origin, and therefore devoid of minerals. As the nights are seldom free from frost, farming is an impossibility, *although flowers grow luxuriantly*."[60] People came to Yellowstone to enjoy the park's scenery, wildness, and tourist facilities, and to be taken in by the spirit of the place. And, people came to Yellowstone prepared to describe the park in a particular way. The typical tourist, after reading the Dunnell letter, may have agreed that Yellowstone was useless for agricultural and other utilitarian purposes, but such thoughts were not necessarily forefront in his or her mind. To the majority of the park's public, Yellowstone was not worthless; it was prized beyond measure.

By the turn of the century, a wide variety of written information about Yellowstone was available to the public. Three railroads boasted that their lines provided the best route to the park. Various stagecoach lines promised luxury service from railheads through the park. And tour companies begged for the chance to organize people's grand tours of Yellowstone as well as points north, south, east, and west of the park. Each of these concessioners flooded the mail, travel offices, and newsstands with promotional and informative literature. In the early decades of the 1900s, several new guidebooks appeared such as Hiram Chittenden's definitive *Yellowstone National Park: Historical and Descriptive* and Reau Campbell's *New Revised Complete Guide and Descriptive Book of the Yellowstone*. The *Haynes Guide* became the official park guidebook and, with annual revisions, was published fairly consistently until the 1960s. This guidebook—lavishly filled with photographs by F. J. Haynes, the park's official photographer—eventually swallowed up much of its competition.

However, these new sources of information did little to dilute the strong image of the park already created by the language of the discovery accounts and disseminated through older guidebooks. Many members of the new generation of Yellowstone reporters and guidebook authors were reluctant to leave behind the language of the now outdated and outmoded discovery accounts. Some clung to the discoverers' words because they best described the incredible impact Yellowstone can have on people who have not yet grown accustomed to stories of its wonders:

> To the early explorers, in particular, who entered this region before it became generally known, its strange phenomena appealed with an imaginative force which the guide-book tourist of to-day can hardly realize. This may account for the fact that some of these explorers, who have never,

before or since, put pen to paper with any literary purpose in view, have left in their narratives strokes of word painting which the most gifted writer would find it difficult to excel.[61]

Similarly, other guidebook authors in later years looked back with renewed respect for the discovery accounts and realized the original accounts may have been truly the best description of what the park had come to be: "If quoting from the opinions of others as to the beauties and wonders of the park I seem at this time to prefer those of an earlier day, it is simply because a fresh perusal of their writings profoundly impresses me that they who first penetrated these wilds and saw and wrote, have left a descriptive record that has not been surpassed if, indeed, it has been equalled."[62]

If the Yellowstone region was not a true terra incognita to its discoverers, it was to an eager, impressionable public. After being bombarded with stories and illustrations of the Yellowstone region, people from all over the United States and from foreign countries, young and old, common folk and aristocrats, all joined in a familiar chorus when reciting the wonders of Yellowstone National Park. The word pictures drawn by the discoverers filled their imaginations and created for them a new place, a new geographical entity or reality. Subsequent reports would be written, photographs taken, sketches drawn, and articles published, but the original image of Yellowstone—the one introduced in the discovery accounts—persisted and served as a template for further evolution of the public's perception of the place.

3

FOLLOWING IN THE FOOTSTEPS

The evolutionary path of certain elements of Yellowstone's sense of place can be traced over time as they travel from their point of origin in the discovery accounts through guidebooks to the diaries and personal accounts of individual tourists and ultimately into actual park policies and practices. Six locations or features of Yellowstone National Park stand out in Yellowstone's literature as especially noteworthy: Mammoth Hot Springs, Tower Falls, Old Faithful Geyser and other thermal features, the Grand Canyon of the Yellowstone River, the Upper and Lower Falls, and Yellowstone Lake (see figure 3.1 and photographs 5 and 6). Nowadays, these and a few other locations are the major sight-seeing stops on a typical tour of the park. The fact that the discoverers chose to describe these particular features or areas attests to their singular significance even in a land full of wonders and suggests that their attraction has not eroded over time.

MAMMOTH HOT SPRINGS

Ferdinand Hayden's description of the Mammoth Hot Spring terraces is important because neither the Folsom nor the Washburn expeditions saw the terraces. Hence, when Hayden noted that the Mammoth springs "had the appearance of a frozen cascade," it was the first such description to reach the public and was immediately accepted as the definitive description of the terraces. Hayden's frozen cascade analogy appears in most of the early Yellowstone guidebooks and other publications and resurfaces repeatedly in personal accounts as well with no apparent reference to Hayden (or Hochstetter) as the originator.[1]

Archibald Geikie, a geologist, was most certainly familiar with Hayden's reports. Upon visiting the Mammoth terraces, Geikie wrote, "At many points

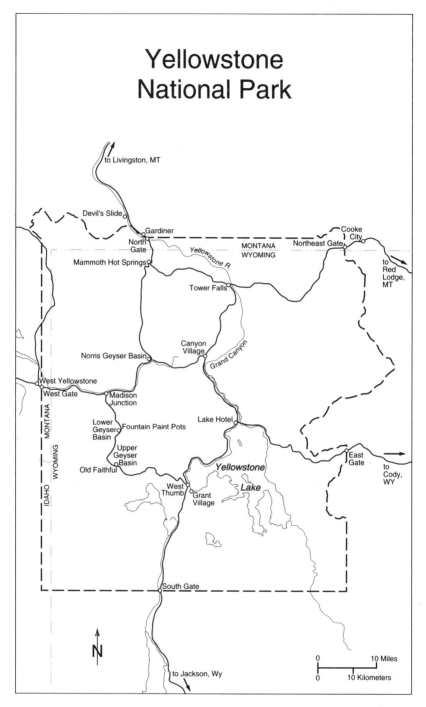

FIGURE 3.1: YELLOWSTONE NATIONAL PARK.
Courtesy of the University of Wisconsin Cartographic Laboratory.

1. THE YELLOWSTONE RIVER SOUTH OF GARDINER, MONTANA. A hike along the Yellowstone River affords a combination of beauty and wildness, recreation and tourism.

2. ERUPTING HOT SPRING ALONG THE FIREHOLE RIVER. Yellowstone is unique in its variety and number of thermal features.

3. The Firehole River above the Falls. All flowing waters in the park are off-limits to water craft in order to preserve these important wildlife habitats.

4. Bison Jam in Hayden Valley. Yellowstone's wild bison herds often "take to the road" causing both joy and consternation among tourists.

5. Mammoth Hot Springs. William Henry Jackson's photograph of the "Stalactitic Basins" in Ferdinand Hayden's *Twelfth Annual Report*.

6. Grand Canyon of the Yellowstone River and Lower Falls. Thomas Moran's chromolithograph, "Grand Cañon of the Yellowstone," in Hayden's *Twelfth Annual Report*. No such vantage point really exists, although a lookout on the South Rim of the Canyon is named Artist Point, supposedly because Moran painted different versions of this scene from that particular location.

IN THE GEYSER BASIN.

7. SIMULTANEOUS ERUPTIONS. In both photographs 7 and 8, the illustrators show many of the major geysers in the Upper Geyser Basin erupting at once. These are most likely fanciful depictions, since simultaneous eruptions are very rare. However, seeing all the Upper Geyser Basin geysers erupt in unison is a comment found throughout the park's historical record and attests to the power of invented traditions. From Stanley's *Rambles in Wonderland* (1880).

8. SIMULTANEOUS ERUPTIONS. From Riley's *Official Guide to Yellowstone National Park* (1889).

9. MORAN'S DEVIL'S SLIDE. Thomas Moran's sketch of the Devil's Slide that accompanied N. P. Langford's *Scribner's Monthly* article of 1871. At that time, Moran had not yet visited Yellowstone and drew from Langford's description alone. Note the symmetry of the sides of the feature and its mountainous setting: both are elements of a belief in nature as sublime and do not reflect reality.

10. THE DEVIL'S SLIDE.

11. MORAN'S GROTTO GEYSER. Moran's Grotto Geyser appeared in Langford's 1871 *Scribner's* article and was based on Langford's description.

12. JACKSON'S GROTTO GEYSER. William Henry Jackson's photograph of Grotto Geyser appeared in Hayden's *Twelfth Annual Report.*

13. GIBSON'S GROTTO GEYSER. In this depiction of Grotto Geyser from John Gibson's 1887 *Great Waterfalls, Cataracts, and Geysers*, the perspective is such that the lone human figure shrinks in size relative to the geyser. Gibson's illustrator probably used W. H. Jackson's photograph of Grotto Geyser as a template for his own drawing (see photograph 12).

14. WARREN'S GROTTO GEYSER. Grotto Geyser in F. K. Warren's *California Illustrated* (1892). In this sketch of Grotto Geyser, the geyser itself does not monopolize the scene so much as provide a backdrop for the human figures approaching it. However, the geyser is still portrayed much too large relative to the size of the people. The drawing of the geyser is basically the same as in Gibson's 1887 work (photograph 13) but more people have been added to the scene.

15. EXPLORERS AT MAMMOTH HOT SPRINGS. Explorers are pictured examining the hot spring formation in this illustration from F. V. Hayden's *Twelfth Annual Report*.

16. TOURISTS AT MAMMOTH HOT SPRINGS. A later sketch of the Mammoth formation in J. C. Fennell's article in *The California Illustrated Magazine* of 1892 shows elegantly dressed tourists added to the same scene as in photograph 15. The explorers are still present but fade into the background.

. . . as one scrambles along that front, the idea of a series of frozen waterfalls rises in the mind."[2] And, frozen cascades appear repeatedly in the poetry of P. W. Norris, one of the early park superintendents. In his poem "Wonderland," Norris wrote:

> Where the azure pools of healing
> Terrace from the snow,
> Like a glist'ning cascade frozen,
> To the glens below.[3]

Another tourist assigned the phrase to all of the park's thermal features by pointing out that "no one can walk around any of the geysers or hot springs in the park without being reminded of ice-formations which he has seen at waterfalls in winter."[4] The analogy even found its way back into the original German—as "Alabaster versteinerte Kaskade"—in an 1895 article in the *Geographischer Zeitschrift.*[5]

    In other parts of his description of the Mammoth terraces, Hayden told of the "wonderful transparency of the water" and the colors of the algae growing in the springs and compared them to "our most brilliant aniline dyes."[6] This passage was so popular, it appeared in guidebooks by Richardson, Stanley, and Strahorn, as did Hayden's description of Mammoth's blue, transparent water that reflected "the sky, with the smallest cloud that flits across it."[7] Lord Dunraven did not cite Hayden as the source of his ideas but suggested that "the water is exceedingly clear, clearer than anything I had ever seen before, and of a blue colour, marvellously beautiful to see. The smallest fleck of cloud floating in the sky is reflected in it."[8]

TOWER FALLS

    Unlike the Mammoth Hot Springs, Tower Falls was seen by the Washburn-Langford-Doane expedition the year before Hayden reached it, and the influence of the previous year's reports on Hayden's interpretation of the falls is clear. In his discovery account, Langford described the rock formations at the brink of Tower Falls as "towers, others the spires of churches, and others still shoot up as lithe and slender as the minarets of a mosque. Some of the loftiest of these formations, standing like sentinels upon the very brink of the fall, are accessible to an expert and adventurous climber."[9] A year later, Hayden wrote: "On the sides of the gorge the somber pinnacles rise up like Gothic spires . . . standing like gloomy sentinels or like the gigantic pillars at the entrance of some grand temple."[10]

Langford's passage was copied in varying degrees by Brockett, Winser, Riley, and Thayer with and without attribution. In a book entitled *Echoes from the Rocky Mountains*—a book about the West generally rather than Yellowstone specifically—the author, John Clampitt, "echoed" Langford when he wrote that "towers, spires of churches and minarets of mosques rise before you and stand like sentinels upon the brink of the falls."[11]

Lieutenant Doane, too, likened the strangely formed rocks to sentinels, but Doane had another, different comment to make about Tower Falls: "Nothing can be more chastely beautiful than this lovely cascade, hidden away in the dim light of overshadowing rocks and woods, its very voice hushed to a low murmur unheard at the distance of a few hundred yards. Thousands might pass by within a half mile and not dream of its existence, but once seen, it passes to the list of most pleasant memories."[12] This passage was used by Henry Norton and L. P. Brockett and paraphrased in books by Robert Strahorn, William Wylie, W. C. Riley, William Thayer, Hiram Chittenden, and Thomas Murphy. However, at the Kepler Cascades near Old Faithful, Doane made a similar comment in his journal: "These pretty little falls if located on an eastern stream would be celebrated in history and song; here amid objects so grand as to strain conception and stagger belief, they were passed without a halt."[13] A combination of these two very similar sentiments found a most interesting expression in tourist accounts. Tourists not only remarked upon the "chaste beauty" of Tower Falls but also developed the idea of how many of Yellowstone's wonders went unnoticed because of the sheer number of other, more spectacular, curious, and amazing sights. Obviously influenced by Doane, another park visitor wrote of Gibbon Falls that "the falls are not wonderful here, but in New England would be justly famous."[14]

OLD FAITHFUL AND OTHER THERMAL FEATURES

Of all the natural features in the park, the thermal features were the most intriguing to the park's discoverers. Here was something new, unusual, and extraordinary—not the typical fare as a subject for landscape description. In the prediscovery as well as in the discovery accounts, six qualities were repeatedly assigned to travel in the thermal areas: (1) a sense of danger or fear of breaking through the crust and falling into the boiling water below; (2) the eerie sound and sensation of walking on hollow ground; (3) a disagreeable smell, usually of sulphur, emanating from the springs or hanging over the basin; (4) a desire to touch the water or rocks in and around the thermal features to verify their existence; (5) a need to stampede or retreat to higher and safer ground when surprised by the eruption of either a known geyser or, more typically, an unimpressive feature not thought to possess eruptive behavior—the viewer usually referred to this experience as having "executed a narrow escape"; and (6) a sense of joy or exhilaration in watching a geyser erupt. Typically, the viewer is physically moved to express himself or herself in some fashion, such as cheering, clapping hands, or throwing hats into the air.

The discoverers' descriptions of specific thermal features made lasting impressions on the readers of their accounts. One of the most popular was Doane's description of Old Faithful Geyser:

> Those who have seen stage representations of Aladdin's Cave and the Home of the Dragon Fly . . . can form an idea of the wonderful coloring, but not of the intricate frost work of this fairy-like yet solid mound of rock growing up amid clouds of steam and showers of boiling water. One instinctively touches the hot ledges with his hands and sounds with a stick the depths of the cavities in the slope, in utter doubt of the evidence of his own eyes. The beauty of the scene takes away one's breath. It is overpowering, transcending the visions of Mosoleum [Moslem's] Paradise; the earth affords not its equal, it is the most lovely inanimate object in existence. . . . Rainbows play around the tremendous fountains, the waters which fall about the basin in showers of brilliants, then rush steaming down the slopes to the river.[15]

Doane's description inspired Hayden to write of the "weird beauty" of the geyser, "which wafts one at once into the land of enchantment; all the brilliant feats of fairies and genii in the Arabian Nights' Entertainment are forgotten in the actual presence of such marvelous beauty."[16]

Doane's fanciful description of Old Faithful as a setting for the play about Aladdin's Cave inspired not only Ferdinand Hayden but guidebook authors, and through them, the public. Norton saw "airy phantoms and ogling water-sprites of mythological tales," while Raymond imagined "fairy caverns" inside hot springs and then told how he "half expects to see a lovely naiad emerge with floating grace from her fantastically carved covert."[17]

Langford's descriptions of the thermal features were especially influential

since they were accompanied by Thomas Moran's sketches—drawn sight-un-
seen—from Langford's descriptions and no small dose of Moran's own imagination.[18] Langford's geyser descriptions had such an impact on Ferdinand
Hayden that he copied many of them into his official report. In the case of
Giantess Geyser, Hayden confessed that since "it has been so graphically
described by Mr. Langford, and so faithfully depicted by Mr. Moran, the artist,
that little more need be added." Hayden assumed that the public was already
well acquainted with Langford's descriptions: "If I should here describe the
Giant, Grotto, Punch-Bowl, and a hundred other geysers of all classes, it
would be pretty much a repetition of what has already been written."[19]

Some guidebook authors used Langford or Doane's description of Giantess (the two are very similar) to describe not only Giantess but other geysers
in eruption. Possibly because Doane also described Giantess as "the grandest
. . . fountain in the world," Robert Strahorn mistakenly assigned Doane's
description of Giantess to Grand Geyser in his 1881 guidebook, copying
Doane's entire Giantess passage and passing it off as his own description of
Grand. The same copying mistake appeared in Brockett and Thayer.[20]

Not only were the geysers' physical appearances described in the discovery accounts but details of their behavior were included as well. The propen-
sity to "salute" was one such common remark. Langford wrote that he and
his party were saluted by the geysers in the Upper Geyser Basin, as did Cap-
tain Barlow: "As we were leaving the valley 'Old Faithful' gave us a splendid
display by way of a parting salute."[21] Later, Colonel John Gibbon wrote: "As
though we were not to be permitted to leave this enchanting region without
seeing it in the very height of its splendor, it is a remarkable fact that, as we
moved along, each geyser, as we passed, broke out in succession, as if giving
us a parting salute."[22]

It is highly unlikely that Gibbon actually saw all the geysers in the Upper
Basin erupt or salute at once. In the winter of 1887, Frank J. Haynes witnessed
and photographed a simultaneous eruption of Old Faithful, Grand, Giantess,
and Castle Geysers. And, on the night of the 1959 Hebgen Lake earthquake,
almost all of the thermal features in the Upper Geyser Basin erupted to some
degree. However, these were rare events and it is doubtful that park visitors
really saw all the simultaneous eruptions that they reported having seen. Nevertheless, from the reports of geyser activity in guidebooks and—perhaps
more important—from the illustrations that accompanied them, early tourists
could easily have come to the conclusion that such activity was the norm.
Hence, as with other mistakes faithfully transcribed into personal accounts,

tourists dutifully documented seeing many geysers erupt at once and included illustrations of the same (photographs 7 and 8). In a passage typical of railroad promotional literature describing the park in anthropomorphic terms— making it seem tame, gentle, and thereby not dangerous or uncivilized—Olin Wheeler, spokesman for the Northern Pacific line, wrote: "From afar Old Faithful espied me, and, recognizing an old friend, trumpeted a salute in his hearty, royal fashion, welcoming me again to his presence. Within fifteen minutes the Bee Hive, not to be outdone in hospitality, did the same, and altogether I felt that I had a *warm* welcome."[23]

In general, guidebook authors incorporated a variety of the discoverers' impressions of the geysers and thermal regions into their own accounts, as-signing certain characteristics to different features or certain experiences to different places. Just as the discoverers immortalized Old Faithful's punctual-ity by bestowing the geyser with its name, so did they endow Giantess Geyser with a feminine beauty as well as the power they recognized might also belong to her spouse, Giant Geyser. Giving human qualities to the geysers and other thermal features was common practice. Geysers typically were said to "groan" or "bellow" prior to the "spasms" of an eruption caused by the feature's "pas-sion," "fury," or "suffering." One guidebook author informed his readers that "there is much individuality found in the geyser family." In fact, "some of them are wonderfully lazy, others have a surplus of energy. The smaller tots and babies are like human children, full of antics. They are impressible, and, like many a young hopeful, "show off" when least expected, are quiet when it is desired that they exhibit their accomplishments."[24]

As mentioned above, the discoverers' observations of the often-danger-ous footing of the thermal basins and the sounds and sensations of treading on hollow ground were popular inclusions in later Yellowstone accounts as was the idea of the narrow escape: "A horseman recently rode too near one of the pools, and the animal, in his terror, broke the crust, releasing a column of sulphur vapor which was almost overpowering. The escape of horse and rider from a horrible death was very narrow."[25] In a letter home to her chil-dren, a wife and mother explained that their father "came pretty near getting a good scald as he peered into the throat of 'Old Faithful,' " and she herself "tripped rather lively over the geyserite surface and pools, lest the boiling water should overtake me."[26] Geyser basins *are* dangerous places and many of the close calls described undoubtedly occurred. But the fact that so many authors chose to include descriptions of such narrowly averted disasters may be a good indication of how deeply they were influenced by the substance of the discovery accounts.

On a brighter and often more humorous note, tourists typically wrote of using the hot springs for washing dishes:

> We are told of a tourist who washed the dishes, his first attempt probably in a lifetime. . . . Pitching the soiled tinware, knives, forks, towels, etc., into a champagne basket . . . unceremoniously dumped them in to soak while he placidly enjoyed his meerschaum. Suddenly, and as if resenting the insult to its dignity, the little spouter spit the basin full to overflowing in a second, setting the contents in a perfect whirl, and the next instant, drawing in its breath, commenced sucking everything toward the aperture. Others at the camp heard an agonizing cry for help, and looking out, beheld the watcher, with hat off and eyes peeled, dancing around his dish pan in a frantic attempt to save the fast disappearing culinary outfit. . . . There would be a plunge of the hand in the boiling water, a yell of pain, and out would come a spoon; another plunge and yell, and a tin plate; and "Oh! ah! o-o-o!—e-e-e!" and a fork, etc.[27]

Robert Strahorn copied this story verbatim from Norton's 1873 guidebook, and the idea soon became a popular one. As attested to by how frequently it appears in the park's written record, washing dishes in the thermal features was one of the favorite housekeeping chores associated with a trip to Yellowstone.

It was not long before the idea of washing clothes in the geysers and hot springs appeared in the public's reading material. At some point, laundering instructions were included as well: "Soiled linen placed in the crater is thoroughly cleansed and uninjured in the process; woolens are, however, destroyed."[28] Those who repeated these instructions were probably referring to a story that surfaced originally in a Robert Strahorn publication, although Strahorn most likely got the story from Norton. A favorite version of this particular story appears in a book written by Carrie Strahorn, Robert's wife, who accompanied her husband on his transcontinental journey along the line of the Union Pacific Railroad. The story as told by Carrie follows:

> Near one of the small laundry geysers sat a workman who had been haying in a meadow close by, and whose facial expression betokened deep trouble. After some questioning he said the boys told him that if he put his woollen shirt in the geyser when it was getting ready to spout that the cleansing

waters would wash it perfectly clean while it whipped it in the air. He had followed their advice and twisting a piece of flannel about three inches square in his finger, he said that was all he could find of his shirt when the waters got quiet, and he said he guessed it had gone down to H—— to be ironed, and he marched off declaring he would "lick them fellers" if they would not buy him a new shirt.[29]

By the time the National Park Service was formed in 1916, washing, cooking, and tossing things in the thermal features were prohibited—as was the generally deplorable prank of writing one's name in the hot pools surrounding geyser formations. However, stories telling of such activities persisted in the park literature, although usually attributed to other people's doings at some past date.

GRAND CANYON OF THE YELLOWSTONE RIVER

The discoverers' descriptions of the Grand Canyon of the Yellowstone River are classic examples of nature writing of the romantic period. They are full of allusions to the sublime in nature, and descriptions of Yellowstone's Grand Canyon have much in common with descriptions of the Grand Canyon in Arizona and the waterfalls and valleys of Yosemite Park, also written during this era. Langford's popular description of Yellowstone's Grand Canyon follows:

The brain reels as we gaze into this profound and solemn solitude. We shrink from the dizzy verge appalled, glad to feel the solid earth under our feet. . . . The stillness is horrible. Down, down, down, we see the river attenuated to a thread, tossing its miniature waves, and dashing, with puny strength, the massive walls which imprison it. All access to its margin is denied, and the dark gray rocks hold it in dismal shadow. Even the voice of its waters in their convulsive agony cannot be heard. Uncheered by plant or shrub, obstructed with massive boulders and by jettying points, it rushes madly on its solitary course, deeper and deeper in to the bowels of the rocky firmament. The solemn grandeur of the scene surpasses description. It must be seen to be felt. The sense of danger with which it impresses you is harrowing in the extreme. You feel the absence of sound, the oppression of absolute silence.[30]

Apparently, Langford's initial experience at the canyon was not unmitigated joy and deep appreciation for the beauty of the scene. Instead, Langford
emphasized—perhaps overemphasized—the painful silence and sense of danger that accompanied his peering into the abyss. Oftentimes, it is not Langford's exact words so much as the sensations he associates with the canyon
that make Langford's description the basis for others' writings. Riley wrote,
"The view altogether is weird and appalling, while the profound solitude and
absolute silence impress the beholder with an overwhelming sense of his own
insignificance."[31] Reverend Hoyt must have been familiar with Langford's discovery account when he composed the following: "Nothing more awful have
I ever seen than the yawning of that chasm. And the stillness, solemn as
midnight, profound as death! The water dashing there as in a kind of agony
against those rocks, you cannot hear. The mighty distance lays the finger of
its silence on its white lips. You are oppressed with a sense of danger. . . . The
silence, the sheer depth, the gloom burden you."[32]

Written in 1878, Hoyt's account first appeared in the nationally circulated literature in 1881 and quickly became an important addition to the
various guidebooks. The passage above was either quoted verbatim or paraphrased in many guidebooks published during the 1880s and appeared in the
Haynes Guides until the 1930s.

If Langford's account—heavily influenced by the language of the sublime—related the size and depth of the canyon to his readers, then Hayden's
account attested equally to its color and form:

> But no language can do justice to the wonderful grandeur and beauty of
> the cañon below the Lower Falls . . . the river appears like a thread of silver
> foaming over its rocky bottom; the variegated colors of the sides, yellow,
> red, brown, white, all intermixed and shading into each other; the Gothic
> columns of every form standing out from the sides of the walls with greater
> variety and more striking colors than ever adorned a work of human art. . . .
> Mr. Thomas Moran, a celebrated artist, and noted for his skill as a colorist,
> exclaimed with a kind of regretful enthusiasm that these beautiful tints
> were beyond the reach of human art.[33]

Hoyt, then, expanded on Hayden's attention to color:

> The whole gorge flames. It is as though rainbows had fallen out of the sky
> and hung themselves there like glorious banners. The underlying color is
> the clearest yellow; this flushes onward into orange. Down at the base the

deepest mosses unroll their draperies of the most vivid green; browns, sweet and soft, do their blending; white rocks stand spectral; turrets of rock shoot up as crimson as though they were drenched through with blood. It is a wilderness of color. It is impossible that even the pencil of an artist tell it. . . . It is as though the most glorious sunset you ever saw had been caught and held upon that resplendent, awful gorge![34]

Reverend Talmage, not to be outdone by a fellow man of the cloth, wrote that the canyon had "triumphant banners of color . . . Sunrise and Sunset married by the setting of a rainbow ring" and went on in unbelievable prose: "Formations of stone in shape and color of call-lily, of heliotrope, of rose, of cowslip, of sunflower, and of gladiola. . . . Wide reaches of stone of intermingled colors—blue as the sky, green as the foliage, crimson as the dahlia, white as the snow, spotted as the leopard, tawny as the lion, grizzly as the bear—in circles, in angles, in stars, in coronets, in stalactites, in stalagmites."[35] Elia Peattie, author of the pamphlet in which Talmage is quoted, concluded his section on the Grand Canyon with, "After this it seems superfluous for me to mention anything I saw or thought in this wonderful country."[36] The public must have accepted such hyperbole, because Hoyt and Talmage's accounts appear almost as often as the discoverers' own words in later guidebooks.

At the Grand Canyon of the Yellowstone, the typical Yellowstone tourist wrote of experiencing many of the same emotions and sensations as Langford and the other discoverers did. Individual tourists told of the canyon's dizzying depth and a feeling of speechlessness, timelessness, and insignificance in the face of God or nature. The painful silence first recorded by Langford was commonly referred to, although in later years, the solemn and terrible silence changed to a reverent hush. Statements like, "We were awed into silence and reverence . . . and we almost felt that we were trespassing on sacred ground," were common.[37] Rudyard Kipling noted that after viewing the canyon, "The maid from New Hampshire said no word for a very long time. She then quoted poetry, which was perhaps the best thing she could have done."[38]

As Yellowstone's record shows, viewing the canyon was often a moving, spiritual experience. And, since mere words often failed to adequately convey the impact of the visual scene, individuals turned to other means of expression: "The long meter doxology was sung at Inspiration Point, the only thing that would in part express what we feel."[39] Reciting poetry or Scripture, singing hymns, capturing the beauty on paper or canvas, or even dancing were offered as attempts to give voice to or to express some idea of the beauty, color, size, and form of the landscape:

My daughter endeavored to produce a water color sketch that would afford
some idea, at least, of the colors; but she found that every stone and rock
required to be painted separately, while the hues were altering with each
change of light, and after working faithfully all the forenoon she gave up
in despair, and said it would require a month to reproduce the scene, even
roughly. She consoled herself, however, for this disappointment by execut-
ing a little waltz upon the little rocky platform from which she had been
sketching, and which projected over the depths of the Cañon, to the
speechless horror of her mother.[40]

Regardless of how they accomplished the task, these tourists all felt the need
to express to others the idea that they had been moved—spiritually, emotionally, even physically (some to tears)—by the sheer beauty of the landscape.
Experiencing the Grand Canyon was—for many people—more than an exercise in tourism. It truly was an experience of the sublime.

This experience of the sublime may have been unique to the Grand
Canyon among other locations within the park, but experiencing the sublime
was not unique to Yellowstone. In the following passage, a tourist described
his reaction to Yosemite National Park's El Capitan:

There are places as well as times and occasions in this world when speech
seems wholly out of place and all talk merest gabble. This was no place for
words here in the awful hush that fell upon us as, all at once, we stood
upon the edge of this fearful revelation. At first sight it was a great horror—a profound abyss, on whose frightful edge we hung . . . terrible in the
grandeur and gloom of its solitude.[41]

Another tourist, touring South Dakota's Badlands, wrote that "an oppressive
silence pervades the dismal solitude."[42]

As geographers, environmental historians, and interested observers, it is
hard to differentiate the language and experience of the sublime in general
from the emotions elicited from viewing Yellowstone's Grand Canyon in particular. It is possible that all descriptions of experiencing the sublime in nature writing is mere linguistic convention. However, descriptions of nature as
sublime and of particular nature experiences as sublime—such as viewing the
Grand Canyon of the Yellowstone, the Grand Canyon of the Colorado, and
the mountains and valleys of Yosemite—should not be discounted or deemed
invalid because they are written in the language of the sublime. Perhaps such
terms do describe best the human response to such scenes. Proof of such is

the fact that the language of the sublime is still in use today in descriptions of natural scenes of overwhelming beauty.

THE UPPER AND LOWER FALLS

On the Yellowstone River at the head of the Grand Canyon are two large waterfalls. The Upper Falls, 109 feet high, is so named because it lies upstream. The Lower Falls, nearly three times the height at 308 feet, is just downstream, hence, "lower" on the river. All of the discoverers described each of the two waterfalls individually, but as important as these descriptions were as sources of information for other accounts, more important was the way the discoverers compared the waterfalls to each other and to the surrounding canyon. Langford began this literary tradition by comparing the waterfalls with the canyon:

> The life and sound of the cataract, with its sparkling spray and fleecy foam, contrasts strangely with the sombre stillness of the cañon a mile below. There all was darkness, gloom, and shadow; here all was vivacity, gayety, and delight. One was the most unsocial, the other the most social scene in nature. We could talk, and sing, and whoop, waking the echoes with our mirth and laughter in the presence of the falls, but we could not thus profane the silence of the cañon.[43]

Later in this same account, Langford pointed out that the "upper fall is entirely unlike the other." What the Upper Fall "lacks in sublimity is more than compensated by picturesqueness."[44] Doane's descriptions of the two waterfalls were less dramatic than Langford's, but Doane added an interesting passage:

> Both of these cataracts deserve to be ranked among the great waterfalls of the continent. No adequate standard of comparison between such objects, either in beauty or grandeur, can well be obtained. Every great cascade has a language and an idea peculiarly its own, embodied, as it were, in the flow of its waters. Thus the impression on the mind conveyed by Niagara may be summed up as "Overwhelming power;" of the Yosemite, as "Altitude;" of the Shoshone Fall, in the midst of a desert, as "Going to waste." So the upper fall of the Yellowstone may be said to embody the idea of "Momentum," and the lower fall of "Gravitation." In scenic beauty, the upper cataract far excels the lower. It has life, animation, while the lower one simply

follows its channel; both, however, are eclipsed, as it were, by the singular wonders of the mighty cañon below.[45]

The following year, Barlow noted that the Upper Fall is the "embodiment of beauty," and the Lower Fall is "that of grandeur."[46] Dunraven characterized the Upper Falls as Langford did, "being more instinct with life, motion, and variety than the other," which is "by far the most impressive."[47] Winser concurred and stated that the Upper Fall "is full of life and action, possessing a beauty peculiar to itself."[48] Winser's description was then copied in Riley's guidebook, and later, in his pamphlets for the Northern Pacific Railroad, Olin Wheeler continued the tradition:

> I confess that to me the upper fall was the greater attraction. There is beyond question a superb spectacle, superiority of power, the effect of crushing, irresistible force, and withal, a stately, noble dignity in the lower fall that compels the homage of the beholder. But there is in the upper fall a life, action, vivacity, energy that are simply irresistible. . . . Rampant with animation and joy, it represents the tireless activity and energy of youth, while the greater cataract typifies the more mature and sedate manhood.[49]

YELLOWSTONE LAKE

Upstream from the falls and Grand Canyon lies Yellowstone Lake. One of the most popular descriptions of Yellowstone Lake first appeared in Charles Cook and David Folsom's 1869 discovery account:

> Nestled among forest-crowned hills which bounded our vision, lay this inland sea, its crystal waves dancing and sparkling in the sunlight as if laughing with joy for their wild freedom. It is a scene of transcendent beauty which has been viewed by few white men, and we felt glad to have looked upon it before its primeval solitude should be broken by the pleasure seekers which at no distant day will throng its shores.[50]

This description of the lake as secluded and pristine appeared in almost all early guidebooks, and Folsom and Cook's original description continued to be cited in annual editions of the *Haynes Guide* until 1947. As pictured in these materials, Yellowstone Lake seemed "civilized and habitable, and is a most restful place after the tour in the infernal regions."[51] At Yellowstone

Lake Hotel, tourists could stop a while and engage in the more usual vacation activities: "Among the Park hotels this is the one the tourist will probably choose if he wishes to remain a few days and rest. Here he can fish, row a boat, go out to the Natural Bridge, lounge among the trees, watch the bears at night . . . or enjoy the splendid view."[52]

All of the discoverers were taken in by the beauty of the lake, "a vast sheet of quiet water, of a most delicate ultramarine hue," but they recognized, too, the severity of storms and the speed with which they arise on the large and alpine lake.[53] Other features of the lake that were observed and made mention of by the discoverers were its shape—which they likened to the shape of the human hand—and the fact that hot springs could be found along the shore in which fish caught in the lake could be cooked. The discoverers warned their readers, however, that trout caught in the lake were usually "wormy." Rossiter Raymond added a bit of humor concerning this latter point when he commented on the ease of catching trout in the lake: "The wormy fellows bit the best, which is strange, when one considers that they have already more bait in them than is wholesome."[54]

HISTORICAL CONTINGENCY AND CHANCE

The events and circumstances that led to the publication of the discovery accounts—the incredible stories told by fur trappers and miners, the collaboration of scientists and explorers, the popularity of the language of the sublime, and the sharing of journals—were a matter of chance. It could not have been predicted that David Folsom, Charles Cook, and William Peterson would trek into the upper Yellowstone River valley in order to verify the tall tales they had heard of the region. Similarly, Gustavus Doane's injured thumb, which required him to copy Nathaniel Langford's journal entries, was not the result of a series of historically contingent events. Hence, the well-focused image of the Yellowstone region that was presented to the public simultaneously with word of its discovery was the result of chance. However, once Yellowstone erupted onto the American scene as a new yet clearly defined "place," a particular course had been set that would determine, to some extent, the future evolution of the park. The creation of Yellowstone as place was not a random event. The sense of place that people would come to associate with the Yellowstone region could not have evolved elsewhere, in another place with another history.

The peculiar characteristics of the discovery accounts both opened up opportunities and formed constraints that would steer the course of Yellowstone's transformation from terra incognita into Yellowstone National Park. Yellowstone's emergence as place, however, is distinct from Yellowstone's origin as the first national park. The origins of the national park idea, like the true origin or discovery of the Yellowstone, may never be known with any precision or accuracy. Not only has the passage of time obscured whatever evidence might lead us to understand both the inception of the national park idea—an idea deeply and strongly rooted in an ancestral, human affection for nature—and the true discovery of the region that was to become Yellowstone National Park, but also it may be that these events have no real origins, no distinct moments of inception. Biological evolution theory suggests that people are generally uncomfortable with evolutionary modes of explanation because "evolutionary stories provide no palpable, particular thing as a symbol for reverence, worship, or patriotism."[55] Yet Yellowstone—despite its hazy origins—has become a place for reverence, worship, and patriotism, and it was the language of the discovery accounts that became both the vocabulary and the vehicle through which Yellowstone's sense of place evolved.

4

THE ART OF YELLOWSTONE

Shortly after the turn of the century, Yellowstone had become a recognized place with traditions familiar to most Americans. The elements of a typical Yellowstone experience found their way not only into textbooks, scientific works, and federal and state government reports but into children's literature and fictional works as well. Ernest Thompson-Seton's children's story of Waub the bear, Herbert Quick's romantic fiction, *Yellowstone Nights*, and Andrew Lincoln's adventure story, *Motorcycle Chums in Yellowstone Park*, were all set in Yellowstone and incorporated the park's features—real or invented—in their story lines. These books—and later movies—perpetuated the discoverers' initial image of Yellowstone. However, it was not only the text of the discovery accounts that made a lasting impression on people's perception of the park as place. The illustrations that accompanied the discovery accounts were copied, embellished or rearranged, and authenticated over time through republication along with the discoverers' words. Hence, the illustrations, too, contributed to the notoriety and immortality of the discovery accounts.

In the United States of the late 1800s, artists began to move away from the landscape art of the Hudson River school. Western artists painted huge canvases depicting the vast, wild, and beautiful landscapes beyond the Missouri River. In fact, for many who would eventually travel west, "reality had been created for them before they ever left home."[1] It was no different for those who hoped to visit Yellowstone. Prior to a trip to the park, one tourist revealed that for him and his traveling companions, "the pictures of Moran have made us impatient to see the wonders of the Yellowstone."[2] The sketches Thomas Moran drew first for Langford's *Scribner's Monthly* articles, then the sketches and paintings he completed to illustrate successive Hayden reports, as well as his own independent works were an especially powerful, attractive force both drawing people into Yellowstone Park and molding their eventual interpretation of it. Moran's first sketches of Yellowstone were drawn before the artist had seen the region for himself. However, the work he did for *Scribner's Monthly* accounts so intrigued him that he joined the Hayden expedition at his own expense the next summer. And, as one of Moran's biographers pointed out, Moran found that in Yellowstone, "actuality . . . was even more bizarre" than some of his imaginative drawings.[3]

These earliest of Moran's illustrations were highly romanticized, more a product of adherence to Langford's exaggerated and romantic descriptions than reality. His drawing of Devil's Slide, for example, was based on Langford's description of the feature rather than an actual sighting (photographs 9 and 10). Of this geologic feature, Langford wrote:

> The sides are as even as if they had been worked by line and plumb—the whole space between, and on either side of them, having been completely eroded and washed way. We had seen many of the capricious works wrought by erosion upon the friable rocks of Montana, but never before upon so majestic a scale. Here an entire mountain-side, by wind and water, had been removed, leaving as the evidences of their protracted toil these vertical projections, which, but for their immensity, might as readily be mistaken for works of art as of nature. . . . In future years, when the wonders of the Yellowstone are incorporated into the family of fashionable resorts, there will be few of its attractions surpassing in interest this marvelous freak of the elements.[4]

Moran's depiction of Grotto Geyser is similarly fanciful (photographs 11 and 12). But, based on Langford's description, it provided *Scribner's* readers with their first visual evidence of Yellowstone's wonders. Langford wrote,

> The Grotto was so named from its singular crater of vitrified sinter, full of large, sinuous apertures. Through one of these, on our first visit, one of our company crawled to the discharging orifice; and when, a few hours afterwards, he saw a volume of boiling water, four feet in diameter, shooting through it to the height of sixty feet, and a scalding stream of two hundred inches flowing from the aperture he had entered a short time before, he concluded he had narrowly escaped being summarily cooked.[5]

Another of Moran's *Scribner's* illustrations revealed his reliance on a source other than Langford's descriptions. Although not included in the originally published versions of the discovery accounts, illustrations of some Yellowstone features were drawn by two Washburn-Langford-Doane expedition members, Walter

Trumbull and Private Moore. These two men must have made their drawings available to Langford and Moran, since Moran's 1871 "Castle Geyser" is almost identical to an earlier sketch by Trumbull and Moore (figures 4.1 and 4.2). Langford's brief description of the geyser—" 'The Castle' . . . has a turreted crater"[6]—is too vague to prompt a drawing with such detailed similarities. Few readers, however, were aware that Moran drew not from experience but from Langford's text, and Moran's sketches gave credence to Langford's word painting. When tourists later saw for themselves the features Moran had drawn, they agreed that Langford's descriptions were accurate.

Moran's later works were a bit more realistic but portrayed the park and park features as mystical, sublime, and instilled with nationalism.[7] Moran's painting of the Grand Canyon and Falls of the Yellowstone River, completed after traveling to the park with the Hayden expedition of 1871, was one of his greatest, most popular works (see photograph 6). Park visitors commonly referred to it in their accounts and were eager to travel to the park so they could compare the painting with the real thing. Typically, their remarks fell into two categories. Either they repeated Hayden's comment that even Moran himself, "a celebrated artist, and noted for his skill as a colorist, exclaimed with a kind of regretful enthusiasm that these beautiful tints were beyond the reach of human art."[8] Or, they chastised themselves for not believing the veracity of Moran's depiction. Almost a century later, William Henry Jackson praised Moran's work by stating: "So far as I am concerned, the great picture of the 1871 expedition was no photograph, but a painting by Moran of Yellowstone Falls."[9]

W. H. Jackson knew whereof he spoke. He, too, was a Yellowstone artist. Hayden used Jackson's photographs liberally in his government reports, especially in the annual report of 1883. Hayden felt that the visual evidence provided by Jackson's photographs would lend validity to his reports, since photographs were considered a more objective representation of reality than were sketches and paintings.

William Henry Holmes, "perhaps the greatest artist-topographer . . . that the West ever produced," accompanied the Hayden Surveys of 1872 and 1878 primarily as a geologist but subsequently as an illustrator.[10] Holmes's sketches filled the pages of Hayden's two later Yellowstone reports and were used extensively by guidebook and other authors as the basis for their own illustrations.

During the park's first decade and long before the invention and introduction of portable cameras, the number of existent pictures of Yellowstone was limited. Hence, most early illustrations found in popular magazines and books were either exact or modified copies of the original works by Moran, Jackson, and Holmes. Often, the same picture appeared in a variety of sources

FIGURE 4.1: TRUMBULL AND MOORE'S CASTLE GEYSER.
This drawing of Castle Geyser by Walter Trumbull and Private Moore of the Washburn-Langford-Doane expedition of 1870 was not published until 1905 when Langford included it in the appendix of his book *The Discovery of Yellowstone Park*. Langford surely must have shown the drawing to Moran, however, since Moran's sketch of Castle Geyser for Langford's 1871 *Scribner's* article is strikingly similar.

FIGURE 4.2: THOMAS MORAN'S CASTLE GEYSER.
"Crater of the Castle Geyser" in Langford's 1871 *Scribner's Monthly* article.

with only slight modifications depending on the purpose or intended audience of the publication. For example, in the book *Great Waterfalls, Cataracts, and Geysers*, Grotto Geyser was portrayed as unrealistically large, dominating the landscape (photograph 13).[11] The illustrator probably copied Grotto Geyser from Jackson's photograph of the feature and then added human figures. The people were drawn disproportionately small, however, which served to exaggerate the size of the geyser. This same view of Grotto was used as the basis for illustrations in other books, among them books by F. K. Warren and by Hezekiah Butterworth whose illustrators added even more human figures engaged in various tourist activities (photograph 14).[12]

In another example, an early drawing of Mammoth Hot Springs was used as a template for a later illustrator's work (photographs 15 and 16). The explorers in the original drawing were joined in the later drawing by smartly dressed, genteel tourists, giving the impression that the park was no longer a wilderness but a modern, civilized tourist resort. In a 1903 *Century* magazine article written by Pulitzer Prize–winning Ray Stannard Baker and illustrated by Ernest L. Blumenschein, cartoonlike caricatures of tourists were added to an otherwise realistic scene of the Mammoth terraces.

In the park's early years, book and magazine publishers faced a paucity of authentic illustrations depicting park features as well as a general lack of knowledge about the park. Some authors and editors betrayed their unfamiliarity with the park by including incorrectly labeled illustrations. For example, F. K. Warren's *California Illustrated* contained a chapter on Yellowstone National Park wherein illustrations of Giant Geyser appear three times in unrelated portions of the chapter. First, an illustration of Giant Geyser taken from an 1880 book by Stanley was introduced on page 120 as "The Giant Geyser." Four pages later, the drawing Moran made for Langford's *Scribner's* (but drawn with help from Moore and Trumbull's sketch) was included but with the caption, "Mud Volcanoes." Finally, an illustration of Giant taken from Hayden's *Twelfth Annual Report* and labeled "Giant Geyser in Action" was added on page 132 in Warren as "A Sudden Eruption." The fact that Warren used three views of the same geyser with different captions indicates he either failed to recognize the different views of the same geyser, or, he had only a small number of geyser illustrations from which to make his illustration selections for the Yellowstone chapter.

Some authors and illustrators added to the developing Yellowstone mystique by designing their own compositions from illustrations that were poorly or incorrectly drawn from the start. Photograph 17, taken from Hayden's *An-*

nual Report of 1878—a supposedly scientific document—showed an imaginary, almost mythological, figure standing at a highly abstracted Mammoth Hot Springs. More than a decade later, the illustrator for Butterworth and Warren redesigned this original sketch, added another view of the terraces in the background, and included it in his image of the terraces (photograph 18; see also photograph 5).

The early art of the Yellowstone—the sketches, photographs, and chromolithographs that accompanied the discovery accounts—were as important in creating the public's image of Yellowstone as "place" as was the language of the discovery accounts. Both were incorporated into subsequent Yellowstone publications and quickly diffused through newspapers, magazines, travel brochures, and books into homes, libraries, and travel offices across the nation and into Europe. Over time, the original image of Yellowstone would be modified, but the shadow cast by the discovery accounts was a long and distinct one. People have always come—and probably always will come—to Yellowstone "preprogrammed" to encounter, interpret, and describe the park in particular ways. However, such expectations do not preclude fascination and surprise. Even today, when so much has been written, painted, photographed, and filmed about the park, most tourists still find something about Yellowstone that is a surprise: "There is in all of us a need to wonder, to discover, and Yellowstone has more than its share of such moments. Each time an animal shows, or a geyser erupts, or the sun shines in a particular way. Each is new and now and gone. No wonder we try to lock these moments away in our hearts."[13] In Yellowstone, "it cannot be said that 'Expectation fails where most it promises,' for it is well-nigh as impossible to exhaust as it is to describe the wonders and surprises of the Yellowstone Park."[14]

At the time the discovery accounts were published, the American public was willing to believe almost anything about Yellowstone that was set before it in print—especially if written by distinguished scientists and explorers, corroborated in the popular press, and confirmed by the sketches, paintings, and photographs that accompanied these written materials. Hence, from its inception, the emerging identity of the park was vivid, colorful, and detailed and would endure for generations, modified rather than replaced by time. Through repetition and wide dissemination, elements of the discovery accounts eventually became real. Hence, our shared image of Yellowstone National Park today grew out of the serendipitous circumstances surrounding the publication of the discovery accounts and the cascading impact of those first impressions and images.

5

EXPERIENCING YELLOWSTONE

The nature parks within the U.S. National Park System are protected from consumptive use as representative bits of nature, wild landscapes, and wilderness. As such, the national parks serve a broad variety of purposes. They are places for finding solitude, for scientific research, and for endurance testing and exercise. National parks exist in order that people can have places where they can be inspired by spectacular landscapes or find moments for quiet contemplation or inspiration. National parks serve as museums and reservoirs not only of endangered and indigenous flora, fauna, and natural resources but of beliefs, faith, and traditions. As the national park movement in this country has evolved, more and more meanings have been attributed to the parks collectively as repositories of nature and nature experiences. Despite these changes on one level, however, people still go to individual parks for reasons based not on modern interpretations of what constitutes a nature experience but for reasons based on the individual park's sense of place.

There has been much discussion in recent decades as to what a national park experience entails, or, more specifically, what sorts of activities should be allowed in particular parks. Questions have been raised as to levels of visitor carrying capacity, dilution of the wilderness experience due to crowding or presence of artificial structures, and the legitimacy or fitness of tourist activities that may have a low ecological impact but are somehow inappropriate (helicopter rides in Yellowstone or hang gliding in Yosemite, for example). When considering the various purposes national parks have served over time, outdoor recreation might appear at first to be a new purpose, one that has appeared only recently due to national changes in lifestyle and popular taste. Travel to Yellowstone for the purpose of recreating, however, is an idea that can be found expressed throughout the historical record. At the turn of the century, the only recreational activities park visitors expected park managers and administrators to provide were those associated with touring the park: horseback riding, driving, or walking, "taking a cure," or merely experiencing a change of scenery or change of pace. Nowadays, Yellowstone recreational activities include everything from mountain climbing and backpacking to sailing, watching movies, and soaking in hot tubs. Certainly, the public's perception of Yellowstone as a place for recreation has evolved from a simple idea—albeit one full of possibilities—into a complex and often controversial reality. But this evolution can and should be characterized as one wherein new meanings have been added to or incorporated into old ones rather than replacement of old ideas with new ones.

From the moment of its inception, the national park was to be a place for people, or more specifically, tourists. In a speech advocating Yellowstone's designation as a national park, N. P. (Nathaniel Pitt) Langford (quickly renamed *National Park* Langford) assumed tourist development to be synonymous with nature protection and appreciation. In his lectures, Langford hoped to convince his audiences that "possessing adaptabilities for the highest display of artificial culture, amid the greatest wonders of nature that the world affords, beautified by the grandeur of the most extensive mountain scenery, a few years only can elapse ere the march of civil improvement will reclaim this delightful solitude, and garnish it with all the attractions of cultivated taste and refinement."[1] After the passage of the National Park Act, an editorial in *Scribner's Monthly* applauded the park's establishment stating that Yellowstone's removal from the public domain "aims to ensure that the region shall be kept in the most favorable condition to attract travel and gratify a cultivated and intelligent curiosity."[2]

That same year, Ferdinand Hayden made his second survey of the park, and Frank Bradley was part of the expedition. Even at that early date, Professor Bradley was already considering potential sites for development in the geyser basins along the Firehole River: "If a hotel were to be located in the region, the best place would probably be on the foot-hills on the east side of the river, between the Lower and Upper basins, since cold springs and abundant forage within easy reach would there be combined with dry locations for building, while the wonders and beauties of either basin would be but a short distance off."[3] Hence, in the park's earliest decades, tourist development was not perceived as conflicting with the natural scene so much as complementing it. The act of protecting the park was meant to "preserve so unique an assemblage of wonders to the uses for which Nature had evidently designed them."[4]

TOURING THE PARK

Although no money was allocated for Yellowstone's management in the original enabling act, park officials as well as the public soon came to believe that funds were needed to make the park accessible. Money was "greatly needed for the development of what nature has lavishly provided for the enjoyment of the people."[5] It was assumed that roads, bridges, and hotels would enhance the park, making it more accessible to those who wanted to experience nature. One tourist who traveled through the park by stagecoach suggested that spending money to improve park roads "would cost the rich Uncle [Sam] quite a bill but it might be the means of securing what is greatly needed for the development of what nature has lavishly provided for the enjoyment of the people. It would be more sensible than much of the expensive display at banquets and funerals and public gatherings in Washington, and cost less."[6] Travel literature proudly featured photographs of the park's hotels, modern roadways, and bridges, all of which were considered feats of human architecture and achievement and suitable companion pieces to nature's architectural accomplishments (photograph 19). Care was taken that the structures would fit in with their surroundings: a combination of form and function rather than mere utility. Bridges were built to accentuate the visual scene, and hotels provided Yellowstone tourists with a sort of luxury in the park's wild setting. Publications distributed by the Department of the Interior pointed out that "the chief public interest in Yellowstone centered around its spouting geysers and similar uncanny wonders of a dying volcanic region" because these were the least trouble to reach. But, "now that good roads and trails have made this great wilderness accessible, its beautiful forests, trout-filled lakes and streams, and its wild animal populations attract as many visitors as the volcanic wonders."[7]

The very location of hotels in the park reflected the bond uniting tourism with the natural constraints of the landscape. By horse-drawn stagecoach over bumpy, steeply inclined roads and allowing for sight-seeing, weary animals, and meals, a visitor could hope to cover little more than twenty miles per day. Hence, the park's earliest hotels were located a day's travel-distance apart at Mammoth Hot Springs, the Fountain Paint Pots, Old Faithful, Yellowstone Lake, and the Grand Canyon. Today, only two of the original, marvelous old hotels still stand: the Old Faithful Inn and Yellowstone Lake Hotel. However, despite faster traveling times and longer traveling capabilities, the new hotels, cabins, and campsites that replaced their predecessors were all built at the old locations rather than at new, completely different sites throughout the park.

From the time of the discovery expeditions, Yellowstone tourists have expected some sort of accommodations in or near the park. The discoverers found food and lodging in Virginia City, Montana, or at Bottlers' Ranch in Paradise Valley north of Yellowstone before journeying into the Yellowstone region. And, from that point in time on, tourists have come to Yellowstone expecting to find a place to sleep and a nourishing meal. In the park's early years, however, travelers often had greater expectations than reality provided, as in this description of a hostelry just outside the park's western boundary:

> The meal itself was beyond description and once eaten is never to be forgotten, for the stomach will give a lasting reminder. We were given something that looked like meat, but like the trees in Yellowstone Park, was destined never to be hewn. We would have considered it a treat had we been served with a lump of coal, a horse-blanket, a slab of marble or a keg of nails, instead of the misrepresentations that were brought to us, which only served to encourage our appetites but discourage them immediately thereafter. Drippings from the "paint pots" would have made admirable dessert instead of the mysterious petrifaction that was dished out. Sir Benk-art, who has talent as a sculptor, managed by supreme effort to carve his name in the butter as a lasting monument to other wayfarers who might be destined to be caught in the web and meshes of the hostelry.[8]

As soon as the Northern Pacific and Union Pacific Railroads built spur lines to the north and west entrances of the park and invested money in tourist facilities, tourists who had the money could experience a veritable "luxury in the wilderness." The Old Faithful Inn, which overlooks Old Faithful Geyser and the Upper Geyser Basin, was built during the winter of 1903–1904 at the site of earlier hotels. East and west wings were added to the main building in 1913 and 1927 increasing significantly the number of rooms available for overnight stays. Designed by a young architect, Robert Chalmers Reamer, the Old Faithful Inn was built so as to reflect its setting and fit in with both the spirit of the park—uniquely American in its log-cabin-castle style; solid and unrefined yet aesthetically pleasing, modern, comfortable, and affordable—and the nature of its location. The inn was built of native materials: rough lodgepole pine logs cut from the park's forests, massive rhyolite rocks quarried in the park, and wrought iron fixtures forged at the site. Of the Old Faithful Inn, one tourist wrote:

Yet with all this rusticity, comfort, convenience and even elegance are everywhere. The polished hardwood floors are covered with oriental rugs and the furniture is of mission pattern in dark weathered oak. The windows are of heavy plate glass in leaded panes and the furnishings of the bed- and bathrooms are of the best. Yet the rustic idea is carefully maintained; even in the private rooms the walls are of rough planks or ax-dressed slabs and everything is redolent with the fragrance of the mountain pine. Verily, this inn is a pleasant place, set down as it is in a weird, enchanted land.[9]

Today, the Old Faithful Inn is as much a natural component of the Yellowstone landscape as is Old Faithful Geyser, grizzly bears, and the Lower Falls. Despite the fact that government proposals to remove the hotel's additions and turn the old house (the original 1903 structure) into a museum appear regularly, public outcry is always so great that the proposals are always withdrawn. It is the public's affection for this building and its purpose as an inn—not a museum—that has preserved the inn as part of the Yellowstone experience.

The oldest hotel still in use in the park, Yellowstone Lake Hotel, was built with Northern Pacific Railroad money between 1889 and 1891. The hotel was completed renovated in the mid-1980s with the goal of restoring as much of the structure as possible to its original condition and glory. With hardwood floors, custom carpeting, huge windows overlooking Yellowstone Lake, and etched glass doors, the hotel recreates an air of elegance, sophistication, and high society unique to this location in the park. If the Old Faithful area was—and is—a place of rusticity and excitement, the lake area was—and is—a place of quiet dignity and polish.

Although many of Yellowstone's first tourists traveled on horseback or in private wagons and coaches, most arrived by rail and traveled with a group (photograph 20). Hence, in Yellowstone, a tradition of group transportation predates the tradition of campfire talks and the creation of the National Park Service itself. As portrayed in the park's historical record, such public, group travel was not only a means of transportation but a dimension of the park experience in and of itself; and, public transportation continues to be an important part of the Yellowstone tradition.

One aspect of public transportation is the social interaction of group travel. Tourists of the stagecoach era commonly remarked on the camaraderie they enjoyed on their tours: "The true charm did not lie in the drive and scenery alone, but in the conversation as well. . . . The supreme pleasure came from the heart to heart talk among congenial companions."[10] Even John Muir, known for his love of wilderness solitude, remarked while traveling in Yellowstone that "among the gains of a coach trip are the acquaintances made and the fresh views into human nature; for the wilderness is a shrewd touchstone, even thus lightly approached, and brings many a curious trait to view."[11]

In the past, when travel through the park was predominantly by stagecoach or touring cars, an intimacy and camaraderie developed among park visitors sharing a conveyance. Contests arose among the different groups as they met each other at points of interest or passed each other over the course of a day's touring. In a similar fashion, flashing lights, honking horns, or a flutter of waving hands nowadays signals the approach of a rival group traveling together by bus or van through the park. In the past, as one woman recorded in her diary, sounding a spirited cheer was not uncommon: "We had company again this evening. One crowd passed us giving the 'Montana Yell' so we fixed one up for our use on special occasions. It is 'Bear! Bear! Eat'em up alive! Wyoming! Wyoming! Nineteen Five!' "[12] The friendships and allegiances that developed within groups as well as the act and art of traveling became for many a most memorable part of their Yellowstone experience.

Some might argue that a group tour detracts from people's experience of the park, since attention is focused on what is happening inside the vehicle rather than outside in the park. But such criticisms arise from a perspective that assumes tourists must appreciate only the nature in the park rather than the nature of the park experience. Throughout the park's literary record there is evidence of how people-oriented a Yellowstone park experience can be:

> While jogging along, our attention was attracted by vociferous singing in the rear. "Can these be cowboys on a spree?" one of the ladies anxiously asked. Soon there emerged from a dust cloud a four-horse stage, laden with a full cargo of clerical gentlemen, of no particular denomination, but smooth shaven and stout, who apparently were not paying the slightest attention to the scenery, but were making the woods fairly rattle with Sunday-school hymns.[13]

The idea of travel—not just moving from one destination to another but an appreciation for the act of traveling itself—is rooted deeply in Yellowstone's past, and one element of this travel phenomenon is the importance of the driver of the stagecoach, touring car, or tour bus. For example, in a Union

Pacific advertisement, the railroad's promoter tells of the difficulties of driving the park's mountainous roads and then asks, "How much more satisfactory to leave such things to a bus driver, who not only is thoroughly familiar with the roads in Yellowstone, but who is also an encyclopedia on the park and can point out and explain things of interest along the way!"[14] The affection and appreciation tourists come to feel for their driver and guide is strongly voiced in the park's written record. For many, especially Yellowstone tourists from overseas, the stagecoach drivers epitomized their beliefs about the American West. A woman from England wrote, "Our driver . . . combined the independence of America with the civility of Europe."[15] Americans, eager to believe their own myths, endowed their driver/guides with qualities and characteristics they may or may not have actually possessed: "A young fellow of the refined cowboy type approached me. A very trim figure was his; the broad-brimmed, grey felt hat of the plains hung upon the back of his head like a Byzantine halo; his features were clean-cut, his complexion fresh and fair; his eyes calm, yet earnest."[16] Rudyard Kipling, disdainful of the American tourist generally, may have empathized with the driver of his stagecoach as he related a conversation that passed between them: " 'I drive blame cur'ous kinder folk through this place,' said he. 'Blame cur'ous. 'Seems a pity that they should ha' come so far just to liken Norris Basin to Hell. 'Guess Chicago would ha' served 'em, speaking in comparison, jest as good.' "[17] Even today, the tour bus driver or guide is an integral part of the park experience for many tourists.

In many ways, much of the Yellowstone travel experience has changed since automobiles have allowed people to travel independently. Tourists in private cars need not stop only at those places the tour company considers important nor need they stay at prearranged overnight stops. Instead, they can tour the park at their own pace and discretion. It is questionable, however, if the independent tourist has more of a Yellowstone experience than those opting for a group tour, despite the independence of the former. Individuals participating in group tours may spend more time actually "taking in" the park than do many visitors traveling on their own. The search for parking spaces, service stations, and answers to questions about the park and its natural features often detracts from an experience of the park itself. Hence, for some tourists, their strongest memories of Yellowstone National Park are not of the park or its particular features but of the frustrations of driving: traffic jams, potholes, and the lack of parking spaces at "must see" sights.

Yellowstone's historical record reveals that the quality of park roads and travel conditions in general has long been a point of contention. In a passage typical of the lighthearted Carrie Strahorn—in contrast to her overzealous and ever business-oriented husband Robert—she described a noteworthy sight on her travel through the park: "A signboard attracted our attention. It just gave the name of the plateau, but underneath some one who had evidently tried Colonel Norris' favorite road with a buggy, had added in pencil: 'Government appropriations for public improvements in the park in 1872, $35,000. Surplus on hand October 1, 1880, $34,500.' "[18] Carrie was not alone in remarking on the poor quality of park roads. In a book entitled *A Merry Crusade to the Golden Gate*, the author recounted the adventures of a group of the Knights Templar from Allegheny, Pennsylvania, who toured the park on their way to San Francisco late in the summer of 1904. Apparently, roads were bumpier and the stagecoach less able to contain its passengers than the knights had expected:

> Amid the clashing of the mustangs' hoofs, the yells of the driver and the report of the whip lash, any announcement that Gilland might have made was lost in the air. Fortunately, another member of the party noted our brother Sir Knight's hasty and sudden departure and induced the driver to halt long enough to gather him in. Happily, Sir Gilland was uninjured and now glories in the distinction that he is the only member of our party who saw that country during "the fall," and declares that he was more deeply touched by nature in that vicinity than any of his brother Sir Knights.[19]

Not only the roads but the dust plagued early park travelers. In an interview, a woman who had toured the park in her youth explained that

> the roads were full of dust around the Basin and mother had been warned that we were not to wash our faces in the park because of the dust. She made us a supply of some kind of softening water that she used. For lipstick we used the inevitable mutton tallow that was a cure all for chapped lips. . . . The dust would gather on the wheels of the wagons and as we would go on it would spill out. The horses would kick up the dirt. When the wind was in the wrong direction we were just nearly smothered.[20]

Especially for those who saw in Yellowstone a symbol of national pride, the dustiness and poor condition of park roads was a national disgrace:

> Everyone knows how roads in Europe climb the steepest grades in easy curves, and are usually as smooth as a marble table, free from obstacles, and

carefully walled-in by parapets of stone. Why should not we possess such roads, especially in our National Park? Dust is at present a great drawback to the traveler's pleasure here; but this could be prevented if the roads were thoroughly macadamized. Surely, the honor of our Government demands that this unique museum of marvels should be the pride and glory of the nation, with highways equal to any in the world.[21]

Eventually, park roads were sprinkled with water to reduce the dust and tourists responded approvingly: "Sprinkling from heavy, wide-tired wagons . . . keeps down the dust and packs and smooths the road, for which the tourist is profoundly grateful to Congress and to everybody connected with the improvement."[22] And later still, park roads were paved and bridges were built making the park even more accessible and easier to travel.

The engineering feats that resulted in the modern-day road system are now taken for granted. At one time, locations that are now regular stops on even an abbreviated park tour were virtually inaccessible due to the inability to cross a river. But tourists of an earlier age were not to be stopped by a little water. Many merely "difficult"—as opposed to "treacherous" or "impossible"—river crossings were typically attempted whether or not a road or bridge existed:

> Our road was a meandering one, as you will see when I tell you that we forded the last fork of Fire-Hole River five times, Willow Creek once, Trout Creek once, Alum Creek twice, and, deepest of all, a bayou of the Yellowstone once. At one crossing we gathered ourselves up on the seat and raised all the luggage, expecting the water to come up into the wagon, but we went through high and dry. I used to be afraid of such doing, but it does no good here; nobody pays the least attention to groans and sighs.[23]

Road building, even on dry land, was not easy in Yellowstone. The park's thick forests required much clearing before roadbeds could be constructed properly. Trees were cut along the routes that would eventually become main roads, but the stumps typically remained for years before further road-building efforts removed them. In the following, a traveler comments on both the water and land crossings during his Yellowstone tour:

> The first section of stumps was about eighty rods long. It was a sort of foretaste of the bliss that was to follow. . . . The coach began to rise and fall in the most unexpected manner. Up and down, crash! whang! bang!

they went. I forgot that [other passengers] were in the coach. I forgot all about the other coach. I forgot about the Yellowstone Park. I nearly forgot my own name. I distinctly remembered, however, that I was in the coach. . . . The carriage-wheels were cutting the most singular antics as they flew over stumps of both low and high degree. I soon discovered that I was not resting upon the carriage-seat but a small portion of the time. The balance of it was occupied by myself in rising and falling; not graceful, perhaps, but forceful I am confident. . . . When that section was passed there was a change. This was of itself a relief, but it was change from bad to worse. We were floundering in a mud-hole so deep that the bottom had not been reached. . . . My only inspiring or consoling thought during that ride was my life insurance.[24]

Today, there exists in Yellowstone a modern highway system, complete with exit ramps and a cloverleaf interchange. In an environment as extreme and severe as Yellowstone's, however, the elements—whether rain, snow, intense heat or cold, geothermal activity, or earthquakes—keep road crews busy all year. After a century of road building and maintenance, complaints about the quality of park roads are still common. Some solace might be taken today in the knowledge that Yellowstone's travel conditions have always been less than ideal.

Perhaps the slower and more deliberate travel of a century ago encouraged an appreciation for the totality of the park experience, which is more difficult to recognize today. At one time, the very process of getting from one place to another—encountering the difficulties as well as enjoying the sights—was part and parcel of "doing" Yellowstone. And, the sequence or direction of the route through the park was important for proper appreciation of the park:

> The route that should be followed in taking the trip is important. The tourist should not visit the points of greatest magnificence first; for then he would be in no mood to enjoy places of minor interest, seen last. Any one of the geysers, if located in Central Park, New York, would attract tens of thousands of visitors, and it would be regarded as one of the wonders of the world. Yet some of these geysers are much finer than others. They are not all in the same locality, but are scattered over a considerable area. To the majority of those who come hither, the cañon of the Yellowstone is doubtless the most wonderful location in The Park; and they should not visit it, till they have first seen and enjoyed things less interesting.[25]

The various railroads that carried tourists into the Yellowstone area incorporated into their promotional literature the idea that the sequence with which
one viewed Yellowstone's wonders was vital to one's enjoyment of the whole
trip. The Northern Pacific Railroad—whose trunk line ended in Cinnabar,
Montana, at the park's north gate—naturally advocated a circular route beginning and ending at the north entrance:

> First, the Mammoth Springs . . . it gives the tourist a wonderfully satisfied
> feeling to behold this marvelously beautiful wonder upon his very entrance
> to Wonderland. He is at once possessed with a satisfied feeling, confesses
> that he feels repaid already for the expense and trouble of the trip, and he
> is started on from here with a satisfied air.
>
> Next, in their order are Rustic Falls, Obsidian Cliff, Lake of the
> Woods, Norris Geyser Basin, Paint Pots, Monument Geyser Basin, Gibbon
> Cañon, Gibbon Falls, Lower Geyser Basin, and the last, the great crowning
> point of all wonders, the Upper Geyser Basin. By this time the tourist
> experiences a full sense of satisfaction, so far as the *wonderful* is concerned.
> He feels a strong desire to witness what in the Park may be classed more
> accurately under the head of the grand and beautiful; so he is taken across
> to the Lake. He experiences a sense of relief at getting away from the odor
> and sight of so much hot water. From the rest and quietness at the Lake,
> he is taken to the great Falls and Grand Cañon. Here the sensation is that
> of *quiet* wonder and amazement, while at the Geysers it is that of *excited*
> wonder and *delight*. At the former place he desires, as he beholds, neither
> to speak nor be spoken to; while at the Geysers he cannot himself refrain
> from shouting.[26]

Naturally, the Union Pacific—whose spur line necessitated a long stagecoach
ride to the park's western entrance—boasted that for maximum enjoyment, a
grand loop tour should start at the west gate. Whether to build suspense or
expectations or to provide relief or inspiration, the sequence of visiting each
part of the park tour was but one element of a grander whole.

Not only was the sequence of travel important, but the time involved
was crucial as well. Even in a time when the typical "package" tour of the
park took anywhere from a week to ten days due to the slow pace of the
horses, Yellowstone Park prophets and advocates warned tourists to slow down
in order to take in the essence of the park. One of John Muir's most often
quoted passages refers to his observation that time is necessary to truly appreciate all that a place like Yellowstone offers:

Few tourists, however, will see the Excelsior in action, or a thousand other interesting features of the park that lie beyond the wagon-roads and the hotels. The regular trips—from three to five days—are too short. Nothing can be done well at a speed of forty miles a day. The multitude of mixed, novel impressions rapidly piled on one another make only a dreamy, bewildering, swirling blur, most of which is unrememberable.

Far more time should be taken. Walk away quietly in any direction and taste the freedom of the mountaineer. Camp out among the grass and gentians of glacier meadows, in craggy garden nooks full of Nature's darlings. Climb the mountains and get their good tidings. Nature's peace will flow into you as sunshine flows into trees. The winds will blow their own freshness into you, and the storms their energy, while cares will drop off like autumn leaves.[27]

Put more succinctly—although less poetically—is the comment from John Stoddard that "the fact that it is possible to go through the Park in four or five days is not a reason why it is best to do so."[28] As roads improved and travel through the park became more and more efficient, the pace of travel sped up accordingly. Over half a century ago, Sterling Yard noted: "One cannot see Yellowstone in a week, although round-trip tourists hustle through it in motor busses in four days and a half. They don't see it; they glimpse it. . . . See the 'sights,' of course, and then see Yellowstone. How? Live in it. Live it. You will have the greatest experience of your life."[29]

Automobiles were first used in Yellowstone National Park in 1915. After two years of competition with horses and stagecoaches, the automobile replaced the horse entirely. At that same time, in 1916, the National Park Service was established. Both events forever changed the way in which people would experience the park. The creation of a national agency whose role it was to manage a system of parks meant that Yellowstone, unique though it may be, moved from being a singular vacation destination to being one stop on a tour of several national parks. And, the arrival of the automobile in the park allowed individuals and families to travel independent of a tour group, tour schedules, and a stagedriver who doubled as tour guide. Tourists could travel quickly and in comfort and isolation from sounds, smells, and sensations *between* park locations.

Guidebooks for Motorized Tourists

Although Yellowstone guidebooks or manuals for tourists changed little during the park's first half-century, the number, content, and format of guidebooks changed rapidly during the 1920s as a result of both automobile traffic and the new, unified, national park administration. Whereas Yellowstone's early tourists had few guidebooks to choose from, modern tourists may find themselves overwhelmed by the number of guidebook choices. Many national organizations—the National Parks and Conservation Association, the National Park Service, the American Automobile Association, for example—all publish their own versions of national park guides as do individuals, scientific organizations, commercial publishers, and local merchants. This variety of materials has led to diversification and specialization. There are guidebooks that consist solely of photographs, a few maps, and an occasional descriptive sentence or paragraph (oftentimes excerpted from a discovery account). There are general guidebooks that point out particularly scenic or interesting sites within the park and offer information as to the location of gas stations, restrooms, restaurants, and overnight accommodations. Others concentrate on the birds, fish, hot springs bacteria, geyser activity, or history of Yellowstone glaciations. There are video and audio cassette tapes narrated by a celebrated cast of popular faces and voices, which can be purchased in the park, through the mail, or in almost every reputable bookstore in the nation. Hence, park visitors have many more options available to them today in their choice of preparatory reading material.

Today's availability of a greater number of Yellowstone guidebooks on a greater number of narrowly defined topics, however, creates a situation where no single guidebook can give its readers a sense of the *whole* park, its sense of place. Yellowstone geology manuals, for example, rarely devote much space to park history or wildlife. On the other hand, wildlife or ecology manuals often neglect to inform their readers of the unique geological features or history of events that first drew the nation's attention to the place and precipitated its designation as a wildlife preserve.

A wider variety of guidebooks has allowed a broader appreciation of the park's many faces, but it may be that with the diversification, something integral—an appreciation for the sense of the place—may have been lost. For example, in the 1907 and 1908 editions of the *Haynes Guide*, Congress Pool—a thermal feature in Yellowstone's Norris Geyser Basin—was described in the following manner:

> The first sight that attracts the visitor is this immense boiling spring, in close proximity to the road, on the left as you enter the basin. It is the largest spring of its class found in the Geyser Basins and is rapidly ap-

proaching a geyser. Its pale blue water is in a state of violent agitation, with occasional demonstrations that force the water fifteen or twenty feet above the rim of the crater; the diameter of the same is fully forty feet. For several years there existed near the Congress the "Steam vent," one of the features of this basin. It consisted merely of an opening in the rocks from which a great quantity of steam was constantly escaping; the roaring of the same could be heard for miles. During the winter of 1893 the "Steam vent" ceased and the Congress appeared. The first eruptions were of great force and completely blockaded the road with masses of earth and formation.[30]

Forty years later, the following described the same feature in the *Haynes Guide*: "**Congress Pool** next to the road, usually a boiling muddy pool, sometimes a steam vent, or is quiescent."[31] The *Haynes Guide* entry for the Fountain Paint Pot changed similarly over the years:

In the basin is a mass of fine, whitish substance which is in a state of constant agitation. It resembles some vast boiling pot of paint or bed or mortar with numerous points of ebullition; and the constant boiling has reduced the contents to a thoroughly mixed mass of silicious clay. There is a continuous bubbling up of mud, producing sounds like a hoarsely whispered "plop-plop," which rises in hemispherical masses, cones, rings, and jets.[32]

By 1949, the mudpot's description was reduced to the following: "**Fountain Paint Pot** is a large hot caldron of clay, quartz and opal, blending in color from white to pale orange and pink."[33]

Finally, the format of newer guidebooks as compared to older ones reflects similar changes in the Yellowstone experience. Yellowstone's earliest guidebooks were written in the form of stories or travelogues wherein the author led the reader on a journey through a strange and almost magical place. Over time, the automobile-era guidebooks became increasingly a mile-by-mile collection of park information so that travelers could orient themselves by mile markers even after stopping, starting, and changing direction.

The two following entries are taken from the *Haynes Guide*. Both descriptions are of Gibbon Falls, the first appearing in the 1907 edition:

Gibbon Falls, whose waters, tumbling in a foamy torrent down a series of steep cascades on one side of a bold, rocky ledge, and on the other streaming in a thin, shining ribbon of silvery spray from a height of something over eighty feet, fittingly conclude the attractions of Gibbon Canyon.

After leaving the falls the road passes for a distance of three or four miles over a succession of pine-clad terraces until it reaches the valley of the Firehole River.[34]

This second description from the 1949 edition begins with numbers that indicate the distance in miles from the Norris Geyser Basin if traveling south and the distance from Madison Junction if traveling north, respectively:

8.80   5.20   Parking area at **Gibbon Falls**. These falls are 84 feet high and are beautiful both at high and low water.

8.95   4.30   Parking area from which Gibbon Falls may be seen. In the bank above the road is a fine example of glacial drift.[35]

By changing their guidebooks to a "motorist-friendly" format, guidebook authors and publishers did not change the public's image of Yellowstone so much as they reflect a change. Over time, it appears, Yellowstone's sense of place has been dissected into discrete bits. Travel through the park can be calculated (to two significant digits if the mileage numbers are valid!), methodically organized, and enjoyed in separate, often unrelated, segments. The uniformity in format among national park guidebooks in general suggests that these changes are not unique to Yellowstone. Rather, people's attitudes toward most of the national parks are changing. Instead of perceiving each park as a singular destination, a "place" to come to know, each national park is merely a series of stops on the way to another national park.

Coming to know Yellowstone's sense of place does not require spending an entire summer in the park. And, developing an appreciation for the park's sense of place certainly depends more on the individual tourist than on his or her means of travel or actual time spent in the park. However, attempts to make travel through the park ever-more efficient and rapid may, ultimately and unconsciously, deter the general public from "being taken possession of by the spirit of the place."

If anything about transportation and the art of traveling can be learned from Yellowstone's past, it is that park managers need not assume that travel through the park must be particularly easy, comfortable, or speedy. Our love of tradition is still strong in Yellowstone. Despite the fact that more modern, comfortable, and functional vehicles are available, several of the original tour-

ing cars that conveyed tourists through the park have been preserved in working order and are still in use, although not on a regular, broadscale basis. Even
the uniforms of the early drivers have been reproduced to complement the
vehicles and provide a more accurate and complete representation of the
Yellowstone tradition. When dignitaries visit Yellowstone, these vestiges of
the park's past are not only displayed but called into service (photographs 21
and 22). When William Penn Mott, Jr., then director of the National Park
Service, came to Yellowstone to dedicate a building upon the death of Horace
Albright in 1987, he chose to travel—despite the rain—in a horse-drawn
carriage, an act that, in itself, reveals respect for both the park's illustrious
past and our tenacious effort to preserve and relive it.

In recent years, access to public transportation in the park has been
severely curtailed. Over the past decade, the NPS has allowed park concessioners to reduce substantially the number of regularly scheduled bus tours,
because profit margins from providing such services are lower than those of
providing tourists with food and lodging. In this day and age of overcrowded
parking lots, high gasoline prices, and an awareness of the dangers and problems associated with automotive exhaust, such a change in policy has questionable merits, especially since bus service is being phased out in those areas
where it is most needed and most popular: recreational vehicle campgrounds.

Forced public transportation in the national parks is something the
American public has tried to avoid at all costs, regardless of the type of vehicle
used. Before cars were even allowed in Yellowstone National Park, one tourist
remarked that "one and all agreed that the ideal and only satisfactory way of
visiting the Park was by private conveyance, camping at will and being generally independent."[36] An expert on Yellowstone's road system and transportation states that "the most important deterrent to a public transportation system is that the general public simply would not accept this rejection of their
freedom to choose the means and the timetable by which they tour the
park."[37] However, over the course of Yellowstone's long history as a place to
travel, park visitors have always had the option to travel individually and
independently or to participate in group, public transportation. This latter,
important element of the park's sense of place should not be denied to future
generations of park visitors.

"IMPROVING" NATURE

The idea that people belong in Yellowstone has long been a part of the
spirit of the place and extends beyond the development of tourist facilities.

At the time of the park's establishment, attempts began almost immediately to regulate Yellowstone's elk, bison, and predator populations, to control forest fires, and to discipline the park's bears. But attempts to enhance nature did not stop there. Some of the park's first officials tried to "save" features from the natural process of erosion and decay.

P. W. Norris, park superintendent from 1877 to 1882, believed Liberty Cap, an extinct hot spring that sits at the foot of the Mammoth terraces (photograph 23) would soon topple over due to excessive erosion and settling. Norris first tried to strengthen the cone with wooden supports but later devised a more ingenious plan to rescue the extinct hot spring cone:

> It therefore becomes a question of scientific as well as practical interest whether a sufficient quantity of water from the much more elevated Mammoth Hot Springs cannot be cheaply conveyed into the ancient supply-pipe of the cone, if, as seems probably, it is still open . . . it is believed that the terrace-building properties of the water would soon encase this interesting cone with the inimitably beautiful-bordered pools of the terrace formation, and also ultimately surround it with an effective and permanent support. So strong is my conviction of the perfect feasibility of this plan, that nothing but absolute necessity of the use of all available funds for buildings and opening roads and bridle-paths has prevented my expending a moderate sum upon the experiment.[38]

Superintendent Norris was never actually able to begin his work on Liberty Cap, but he did succeed in building a trough carrying hot spring water from active springs at the top of the Mammoth terraces to a smaller inactive hot spring cone near Liberty Cap called the Devil's Thumb. As one tourist wrote of Norris's endeavors: "It is hoped that the deposits of time may gradually fill up the fractures and cavities, and renew the youth of the cones. It would be a pity for these mausoleums of old geysers to crumble to dust."[39] Sketches from guidebooks and other Yellowstone accounts show the trough and Devil's Thumb (photograph 24).

Norris did not hope to rescue Liberty Cap for the sake of proving human strength, ingenuity, and control over nature so much as he was genuinely concerned for Liberty Cap and its importance and meaning to the park and the park experience. When Rudyard Kipling visited Yellowstone in 1889, he remarked on other attempts to restore inactive springs. In the following, Kipling tells of the efforts of a cavalry officer stationed at Mammoth: "He himself was devoting all his time to conserving the terraces, and surreptitiously running hot water into dried-up basins that fresh pools might form. 'I get very interested in that sort of thing. It's not duty, but it's what I'm put here for.' "[40]

Nowadays, in looking back, it is easy to label such policies and attitudes as ignorant of the power and processes of nature, as classic examples of how humans foolishly perceived their relationship to nature as kindly paternalistic, demeaning, or antiwilderness. But a century ago, such behavior was not based on a malicious or arrogant belief that people were superior to nature but that people and nature could coexist. Instead, improving the natural landscape by making it accessible to tourists was considered a fitting and proper way to acknowledge and applaud the park's wonders and naturalness.

ENGAGING IN THE ART OF PLAY

Once tourists could travel to and through Yellowstone without too much inconvenience, site-specific or park-specific forms of recreational behavior began to catch on. One such behavior was "playing." For many, the wild and curious landscape instigated childlike behavior. Even today, after one of Yellowstone's summer snowstorms, it is not unusual to find a group of tourists—senior citizens, no less—stop their tour bus, disembark, and begin a snowball fight. In an earlier day, when there were fewer restrictions on what park visitors could and could not do, tourists actively engaged in the physical, playful games or activities usually associated with children:

> After fully enjoying the scene, we amused ourselves by rolling large rocks over the cliff. It was wonderful to see a stone the size of a trunk leap into the air in a plunge of 200 or 300 feet, strike the shelf below as if thrown by a catapult, and with such tremendous force as to rebound twenty feet, and after a series of such terrific bounds, make another tremendous leap to the slope below, continuing in bound after bound until it reached the creek. . . . While indulging in this boyish sport a faint shout came up from below signifying that there was some one down in the cañon. It is unnecessary to say that we at once stopped the stone rolling.[41]

In many ways, being in the park has always made people feel—or at least act—young. And, an integral part of children's play behavior is its learning function. Most adults lose their need for physical, tactile proof of something's existence. However, the nature of Yellowstone's environment elicits in adults this tactile investigation so necessary to children's learning and maturing processes. The clarity, depth, and color of the water in the hot springs entices people to stick probing fingers into the steaming water, testing reality. Despite rules forbidding such behavior and constant warnings from rangers, tourists automatically pick up rocks and flowers to feel, smell, and examine them. Tourists stop to feed birds, marmots, and ground squirrels and yearn to remove socks and shoes and wade in the pools, streams, and rivers.

Such behavior is a part of the Yellowstone tradition, because Yellowstone is a sensuous place, "appealing at once to sight, smell, touch, and hearing."[42] Along the Yellowstone River in the Grand Canyon, one of the park's discoverers took the time to note the sensations assaulting him: "The river water here is quite warm and of a villainously alum and sulphurous taste. Its margin is lined with all kinds of chemical springs. . . . The internal heat renders the atmosphere oppressive, though a strong breeze draws through the cañon. A frying sound comes constantly to the ear, mingled with the rush of the current. The place abounds with sickening and purgatorial smells."[43] Even the sense of taste is an important part of Yellowstone's sensory environment. Although few tourists nowadays feel the need to sample water from the various thermal features, drinking hot spring water was at one time a typical part of coming to know the place: "I do not distinctly recall all the nasty tastes which have afflicted my palate, but I am quite sure this was one of the vilest. It was a combination of acid, sulphur and saline, like a diabolic julep of lucifer-matches, bad eggs, vinegar and magnesia. I presume its horrible taste has secured it a reputation for being good when it is down."[44]

The thermal areas, especially, stimulated imagination and sense of fun in park visitors. The sputtering of the smaller geysers and the bubbling of the mudpots elicited a variety of humorous and, at times, quite astute observations from their audiences. One popular comment was that the hissing and splashing of Catfish Geyser "is not vastly different from some politicians" in that they, too, "have literally spouted themselves to exhaustion in the effort to shoot a great ball a long distance out of a small calibre."[45]

Although there are any number of landforms in the United States whose names incorporate the words "Devil," "Purgatory," "Hell," "Styx," "Hades," or "Satan," these terms seem especially appropriate in Yellowstone. The physical nature of the park's thermal regions encourages viewers to conjure up images that are other worldly or Hell-like, thereby prompting the park's devilish nomenclature. Also, as if reciting a script, tourists allude to Hell or the "Nether regions," noting the sulphurous smells and bubbling sounds. These references to the devil are not so much somber and sober reminders of our

own mortality as they are intended to be creative, lighthearted, and humorous, as in a description of devilish imps working the plumbing systems of the
geysers and hot springs: "It requires no great flight of fancy to see in this
marvelous natural mechanism a vast engine running under the guidance of a
ghostly engineer, and being 'stoked' from Pluto's wood-pile by a thousand
goblin firemen."[46]

Thermal features, however, are not always referred to in demonic terms.
The park's hot springs, geysers, mudpots, and fumaroles are often personified.
A story repeated throughout the park's history is set in a hot spring basin and
pokes fun at the clergy: "One very large basin (40 × 60 feet) is filled with
the most beautiful slime, varying in tint from white to pink, which blobs and
spits away, trying to boil, like a heavy theologian forcing a laugh to please a
friend, in spite of his natural specific gravity."[47]

Early photographs of tourists show them actively discovering and enjoying the park. Like children on a new playground, they climbed on deposits,
lowered themselves into caves, fed bears, and swam in the hot pools (photographs 25 and 26). The suitability of Yellowstone's hot springs for swimming—especially the pools formed in the Mammoth terraces—is a long-run-
ning debate in Yellowstone's written legacy as conflicting evidence is offered
on this point. In an 1882 account, Mammoth's wonderful baths were praised:
"Toward evening I enjoyed a bath among the natural basins of Soda Mountain. The temperature was delightful, and could be regulated at pleasure by
simply stepping from one basin to another. They were even quite luxurious,
being lined with a spongy gypsum, soft and pleasant to the touch."[48] Similarly, Dr. S. Weir Mitchell sent many a troubled patient to Yellowstone to
cure tired and overwrought nerves. He himself found the terrace baths to be
both enjoyable and serviceable:

> With hundreds of gleaming bath-tubs full of water from 180° Fahrenheit
> down to 75°, the temptation to hot and tired men to bathe was delicious,
> and the only trouble lay in the difficulty of choosing our place. Finally, we
> set our hearts on a noble tub about three feet deep and eight in diameter.
> My friend, being neat in his ways, much rejoiced over the little dry basins
> about us, which he called dressing-tables. In one he put his brushes, in
> another a battered hat; in one soap and sponge, in another clean towels;
> and so on, with little clean nests for shoes and clothing worn or to be
> worn.[49]

During that same time, however, there were those who disagreed and found
the terraces neither comfortable nor practical for bathing: "We cannot leave

. . . without mentioning the hot baths. All over the crusts of the different terraces are, as has been mentioned, small basins containing water of almost any temperature desired; but bathing in these pools cannot be accomplished with comfort, since the pools are almost always too shallow to admit of it."[50]

Despite the complaints, the idea of bathing at Mammoth eventually became firmly ingrained in the national consciousness as part of the Yellowstone experience. Park authorities soon allowed concessioners to build bathing facilities to accommodate the tourists' wishes to test the waters (photograph 27):

> A small tent is pitched a short distance from the main basin, and looking in you find an oblong hole, dug in the pure white soil, large enough to contain the human form. It is full of water, led from the spring through a trough hollowed out in the ground. This is the primitive bathing establishment of the place. They have become more luxurious out there since, and have put up several plank bath-houses, with real bath-tubs in them. The tubs are not made of white marble, nor are the floors covered with Brussels carpets;—these things will come in time. Already, these different bath-houses have established a local reputation with reference to their curative qualities. Should you require parboiling for the rheumatism, take No.1; if a less degree of heat will suit your disease, and you do not care to lose all your cuticle, take No.2. Not being possessed of any chronic disease, I chose No.3, and took one bath—no more. When I recovered I made a mental resolution never, willingly, to be a party to the cruel process of rendering lobsters edible.[51]

For a time, public bathing facilities were operated at Mammoth and near Old Faithful, and fees were charged accordingly: "50 cents in large pool at Old Faithful and Mammoth; $1.00 in private pool at Old Faithful."[52] The private pool constructed at Old Faithful (photograph 28), the Hamilton Swimming Pool, had two pools—one for adults, one for children—and was fed with water diverted from Solitary Geyser.[53] For many decades, swimming and wading in hot springs was a popular part of the Yellowstone experience, but the sheer number of tourists now visiting the park prohibits such activities. Swimming and soaking in the springs was first discontinued when it was found that, rather than being therapeutic, hot spring water can be dangerous, because water temperatures can change quickly and without warning. Further, in keeping with attempts to restore and preserve even the tiniest of Yellowstone's ecosystems, protection was extended to the colonies of bacteria and algae living in the hot springs and their runoff channels, which are destroyed when people walk, sit, or swim in the water. Bathing in hot springs is now prohibited, but visitors can soak in several "hot pots" formed where hot water flows into cold rivers, lakes, or streams.

YELLOWSTONE'S GRIZZLY BEARS

Today, with the exception of Old Faithful Geyser, Yellowstone's bears are probably the most well-known and popular tourist attraction in the park. This has not always been the case, however. Yellowstone National Park was not established as game reserve, although its organic act did call for protection against "wanton destruction" of the park's fish and game. During the first two decades of the park's existence, tourists and concessioners alike hunted in the park for food, and many early tourists came to Yellowstone with the clearly expressed purpose of hunting elk and bear as a recreational activity. But, by the turn of the century, the nation's new concern for wildlife led to legislation protecting all park wildlife, and the thrill and necessity of the hunt was replaced by the comfort and civility of the hotel dining room.

Bears, however, were already immensely popular as a singular attraction. Long before gaining fame and affection as beggar bears lining park roads or waiting for handouts in parking lots and campgrounds, Yellowstone's bears were thought of as tangible evidence of Yellowstone's wildness. Jean Crawford Sharpe, an eight-year-old who spent summers in Yellowstone with her mother who was a social director at one of the park's tent camps in 1909, described some of these early tourist-bear encounters:

> When the fire died down to glowing embers and "Good-night Ladies" had been sung, and it was time to turn in, the timid folk were escorted to their tents by someone carrying a kerosene lantern. (Bears were wary of lights.) . . . Bears were plentiful. Visitors from the east waited in shivering expectancy to see their first wild bear.
>
> This mischievous eight-year-old was often amused by planting her teddy-bear in a tree then seeking out a newly arrived "dude" and saying there was a bear in a tree just outside. Perhaps the dude was not amused at all, but maybe he felt for a moment his first thrill of danger in this wild, wild place.[54]

As bears lost their fear of humans and ventured closer to the easy food supplies available in camp and hotel garbage dumps, concessioners saw an opportunity in staging bear feeding shows. Soon, visitors came to Yellowstone expecting to see bears "in the wild" feeding on restaurant and picnic garbage. Word of Yellowstone's "wild" bears spread and became an important park tradition: "For your interest and entertainment are recreation and dance halls, outdoor pageants, ranger guide and lecture service, horseback riding and nightly bear feeding activities at the bear feeding grounds which here are frequented by a large representation of grizzlies."[55]

Not everyone evinced equal enthusiasm regarding the park bears, however. One tourist voiced a strong—although untypical—opinion when he wrote, "The Yellowstone Park bears are an unmitigated and intolerable nuisance, and nine tenths of them should be killed at once."[56] Others did not oppose the bears so much as the popular notion that they were wild: "Yet the Yellowstone, for all its superb green beauty, is no howling primitive wilderness. . . . These bears are a relic of the wild, but also as authentic a product of man as the domestic horse or the garden rose. It is no easy task to preserve the old America, as the national park directors are well aware, and the bears are one of a series of carefully watched park exhibits."[57]

However, for all their profound insight, these are minority opinions. The majority of Yellowstone accounts suggest that people believe seeing bears to be a valuable, essential part of the park experience. And, although the Park Service has implemented management practices over the past twenty years to reduce the number of human-bear encounters, these policies do not reflect the attitudes of most modern tourists whose expectations of the park are based on Yellowstone's past. People still travel to Yellowstone to see bears:

> Yellowstone's bears are vanishing from view. Not every visitor is happy with this development. I sat for a full afternoon in a ranger station and recorded some of the comments:
>
> "Do you realize I came all the way from New Jersey to see two things—Old Faithful and a real live bear in the open? I mean, look, buddy, seeing a bear running free may not mean much to you, but when you live in Weehawken, it can be a big thing in your life."[58]

FISH STORIES

For some, a few recreational activities have become almost synonymous with a Yellowstone vacation: geyser gazing, seeing bears, and fly-fishing. Compared to geysers and bears, the popularity of fishing may be less obvious. Home to three of the world's best trout fishing streams, Yellowstone has always provided its public with good fishing, but recently, the park has become a Mecca for devout fly fishermen. In the Yellowstone literature, the theme of fishing is woven throughout the historical record. Part of the park's fishing fame stems from the abundance of fish, notably cutthroat trout, and the supposed ease with which even beginners can hook them. Another is the quality of the setting—angling for wild trout in a free-flowing river, either close to the road or miles from the more inhabited parts of the park. As popular as fishing is, however, it is not necessarily every Yellowstone tourist's passion, a point one tourist made very clear to his traveling companions who were avid anglers themselves:

> I am not a fisherman. . . . I fish not, neither do I angle. It's very silly, in my estimation. I never could see the percentage of getting all dressed up in Fisherman's Disguise No.3, debating over an album of synthetic insects and sneaking up on some moron fish with a trusting disposition. . . . I'd get a better thrill casting in the ice-box for a can of sardines and landing them with a Eureka Handy Kitchen Tool, combining the features of both can-opener and egg beater.[59]

"Fishing Cone," a geyser situated in Yellowstone Lake a short distance from shore at the West Thumb Geyser Basin, has a long history as a tourist attraction. Hayden described the feature and included sketches of it in his reports (photograph 29): "The 'Hot Spring Cone' we called the 'Fish-Pot,' from the fact that it extended out into the lake several feet, so that one could stand on the siliceous mound and hook the trout from the cold waters of the lake, and, without moving boil them in the steaming-hot water of the spring."[60] Hayden's reference to the idea of catching and cooking a fish in one place was probably the result of a Jim Bridger story. Jim Bridger, a fur trapper who hunted and traveled through much of the greater Yellowstone area fifty years before the park was "discovered," has been credited with most of the tall tales told of the region. One such tale is that Bridger found a place in the Rockies where so many hot springs poured boiling water into a lake that the hot water formed a thick layer on top of the colder lake water. Being an astute angler, Bridger decided to hook a trout in the lake's cold, deep waters and reel it in so slowly that by the time he pulled the fish out, it was cooked![61]

By the turn of the century, catching a fish in the lake and cooking it in Fishing Cone became a park experience "without which no visit to the Park would be quite successful"[62] (photograph 30). For the well-being of the park's human as well as aquatic inhabitants, however, this practice was deemed in later years "no longer permissible for humane reasons."[63] Nevertheless, the tradition of catching and cooking one's dinner in the same spot was a powerful and popular one—a unique Yellowstone experience—and it quickly spread to other parts of the park. The hot springs along the Gardner River, in an area now referred to as "Boiling River," were also used as the setting in individuals' accounts of cooking-fish-on-the-hook activities. Hence, the Fishing Cone tradition, although it began with one particular hot spring, came to be associated with many different hot spring areas throughout the park.

Stranger still than the origin of Fishing Cone is the shorter-lived but as yet unresolved and unexplained question concerning the eerie overhead noises heard at Yellowstone Lake. In Hayden's second report on the Yellowstone region, a colleague wrote:

> While getting breakfast, we heard every few moments a curious sound, between a whistle and a hoarse whine, whose locality and character we could not at first determine, though we were inclined to refer it to waterfowl on the other side of the lake. As the sun got higher, the sound increased in force, and it now became evident that gusts of wind were passing through the air above us, though the pines did not as yet indicate the least motion in the lower atmosphere.[64]

Hiram Chittenden included a description of this "most singular and interesting acoustic phenomenon" in the earlier editions of his book, *Yellowstone National Park*, and, in later editions, Chittenden cited scientific reports and articles published in professional journals, which described the strange occurrence. In a 1926 *Science* article, Hugh Smith told of his observations:

> The canoe had barely gotten under way and was not more than twenty meters from the shore when there suddenly arose a musical sound of rare sweetness, rich timbre, and full volume, whose effect was increased by the noiseless surroundings. The sound appeared to come from directly overhead, and both of us at the same moment instinctively glanced upward; each afterward asserted that so great was his astonishment that he was almost prepared to see a pipe organ suspended in midair.[65]

Over the years, park visitors have likened the noises to "the ringing of telegraph wires or the humming of a swarm of bees," "a rather indefinite, reverberating sound in the sky, with a slight metallic resonance," and "atmospheric disturbance caused by violent eruptions and the liberation of gases."[66] Even as late as the 1940s, the *Haynes Guide* included a section on Lake's mysterious noises: "These occur when the sky is cloudless, the air perfectly still and usually in early morning. This strange noise, heard only occasionally, is not like the sound of a distant flight of birds nor any shore noise, but is weird and startling."[67] Although many tourists noted hearing the noises, many more simply alluded to them, acknowledging disappointment at having missed hearing them. Others quoted from their guidebooks the fact that the noises do exist. Hence, whether real or imagined, the overhead sounds became part of the Yellowstone experience as stories were repeated, passed on from one generation of visitors to the next.

Today, there are many activities that together constitute a "Yellowstone" experience. Most of these are nonconsumptive or highly regulated so as to both benefit the tourist and lessen the environmental impact. For most modern park proponents and visitors, the idea of "improving nature" with roads, hotels, or predator control goes against current philosophies of wilderness or nature preservation. In fact, the building of roads and tourist accommodations is typically cited as the reason that the national parks are being "loved to death." Historical attempts to provide recreational activities has also been blamed for the degradation of both the Yellowstone experience and the park's natural ecosystems. It should be recognized, however, that many of these activities were undertaken out of love for the park and its features, a desire to experience the park through touch, taste, and feel, as well as a sense of duty and honor in being able to show off the park to the American public and the world. The past should not be judged by modern standards lest we forget the rich heritage of meanings that created and continues to define Yellowstone.

6

THE IDEA OF THE IDEAL

Scholars writing about the evolution of the national parks or the national park ideal are often guilty of operating under the assumption that there is an "ideal" national park.[1] They intimate that the evolution of the national parks has proceeded with an inherent determinism—along with science and a broadening ecological awareness—from a less-than-noble state toward a more perfect national park ideal or goal in nature preservation. And, the phrase "the national park ideal" is commonly used to describe the end-product of a complex and varied history of national interests in nature preservation. Such thinking and terminology creates the illusion that there is, indeed, one ideal or one set of values to which all parks should conform and that this ideal is consistent with modern conditions in and perceptions of the parks.

Little consensus exists, however, among park proponents as to what an ideal park is or what its primary purposes are. Some people travel to the parks mainly for family sight-seeing excursions, while others use the parks for wilderness recreation. Another faction sees the parks as sanctuaries where human intrusion should be limited to scientific studies with minimal human impact and intervention. Even within groups and organizations that support national policies concerning nature preservation generally, dissent and disagreement are commonplace.[2] For Alfred Runte, the real purpose of national parks is to preserve natural ecosystems, and he argues that Yellowstone was not only the first national park, "but, by virtue of its size, it was the first to anticipate the 'ideal' national park as the idea came to evolve."[3] In his arguments, Runte assumes there is a shared understanding of what the national park idea and ideal are. Other park historians, critics, and enthusiasts have also made cases for their own interpretation of the national park ideal. Frederick Law Olmstead believed that providing a setting for contemplation was the highest value served by the national parks, and Edward Abbey was certainly one of the most vocal and radical proponents of viewing national parks as places where one should be able to find life-or-death wilderness experiences.[4] Hence, different people have found different reasons for settling upon one or another ideal purpose for America's national parks, and all argue that the parks should be managed in a way that conforms to their particular and often elusive state of naturalness.

If national park scholars move away from the notion of evolution as progressing toward an ideal, they may put to rest an old and unending debate within their ranks. Management programs based on the notion that there has never been a single national park idea, but rather countless attempts throughout history to preserve and protect natural landscapes—nor is there a single national park ideal, but rather as many ideals as there are parks—may provide the NPS with both the flexibility and consistency it lacks today. If each park is, in a sense, one expression of an ideal national park, park administrators could make decisions based on compatibility with sense-of-place standards rather than "pristine nature" or "intact ecosystem" standards. Such a management philosophy encourages park officials to take into consideration a park's history and cultural richness when designing management programs. Understanding why people were first drawn and continue to be drawn to a region or understanding what qualities form the basis of people's expectations of a particular park experience could help managers find a middle ground based on new scientific information yet compatible with the park's spirit of place.

PERSONALITY AND CHARACTER OF PLACE

Yi-Fu Tuan, a geographer who has written much about the importance of recognizing and acknowledging the power that certain places exert on human thought, emotion, and behavior suggests that the personality of a place can have two faces: "one commands awe, the other evokes affection. . . . The personality that commands awe appears as something sublime and objective. By contrast, a place that evokes affection has personality in the same sense that an old raincoat can be said to have character."[5] An examination of Yellowstone accounts reveals evidence of both the park's personality and its character. Certain places and events in the park command the awe and respect of their audiences: views of the Grand Canyon and the Lower Falls, an eruption of Old Faithful, a windless day at Yellowstone Lake. At the same

Fig. 18.
Ornamented Basins at Mammoth
Hot Springs of Gardiner's River.

17. MYTHIC FIGURE AT MAMMOTH HOT SPRINGS.
Sketch entitled "Ornamental Basins at Mammoth Hot Springs of Gardiner's River" from F. V. Hayden's *Twelfth Annual Report.* The highly abstracted hot spring fountain and the mythical figure may have been included because it was common practice at this time to name natural features for figures from history or various classical mythologies. Different hot springs at Mammoth had already been named Jupiter, Minerva, and Cleopatra Terrace, so this obviously fictional depiction may have been in keeping with the imagery rather than its reality as a place.

18. BUTTERWORTH'S MAMMOTH HOT SPRINGS. This illustration from H. Butterworth's *Zigzag Journeys* (circa 1892) consists of an unrealistic figure and depiction of the hot spring formation similar to photograph 17 but with the addition of another, more realistic view of the terraces in the background. The exact same sketch is found in F. K. Warren's *California Illustrated.*

19. ROADS AND BRIDGES AS "YELLOWSTONE WONDERS." In the Northern Pacific Railway's *Wonderland* 1903 pamphlet advertising tourism in the West generally and in Yellowstone National Park specifically, two of the three features depicted as parts of the "Yellowstone Wonderland" are not natural. The first panel shows an erupting Old Faithful Geyser, the middle panel shows the Chittenden Bridge spanning the Yellowstone River, and the third panel shows the road and bridge through the Golden Gate Canyon southeast of Mammoth Hot Springs. Illustration reproduced courtesy of the Burlington Northern Railroad.

20. STAGECOACHES WAIT FOR PASSENGERS IN GARDINER, MONTANA. Most of Yellowstone's earliest tourists traveled to Yellowstone by rail and, at one time, had their choice of five different rail lines by which to travel. Privately owned and commercially run stagecoaches met train passengers at the railheads and provided transportation through and information about the park. Once private automobiles were allowed to enter the park, touring cars rapidly replaced stagecoaches as the principal form of public transportation. Today, private cars are the primary means of transportation through the park. Photograph courtesy of the National Park Service, Yellowstone National Park.

21. Transportation Traditions. Restored White Touring Cars are still used in the park on special occasions. The drivers' uniforms are exact replicas of the original drivers' uniforms.

22. Horse and Buggy Days. When William Penn Mott, Jr., visited the park in 1988, he traveled via horse and buggy despite the rainy weather, confirming the importance of tradition in Yellowstone.

23. LIBERTY CAP. William Henry Jackson's photograph of Liberty Cap, an extinct hot spring at the base of the Mammoth Hot Spring terraces, appeared in Hayden's *Twelfth Annual Report.*

24. MAMMOTH HOT SPRING TERRACES WITH INSERT OF DEVIL'S THUMB. This sketch entitled "Mammoth Hot Springs.—Main Terrace" from W. M. Thayer's 1891 *Marvels of the New West* shows—in the insert—the trough set up to bring hot water from the active springs at the top of the mountain to the extinct cone named the Devil's Thumb in an effort to reactivate it. Another, larger, extinct hot spring cone, Liberty Cap, is in the foreground of the insert.

25. ENTERING DEVIL'S KITCHEN. Until noxious fumes necessitated closing the spring to the public, tourists regularly climbed down into caves and hot springs at Mammoth. Photograph by F. J. Haynes, courtesy of the Haynes Foundation Collection, Montana Historical Society.

26. BEGGAR BEARS. Grizzly and black bears once lined the roads "begging" for scraps. The picnic-basket-thieving cartoon character "Yogi Bear" from Jellystone National Park was based on Yellowstone's infamous beggar bears. Photograph by Robert McIntyre, courtesy of the National Park Service, Yellowstone National Park.

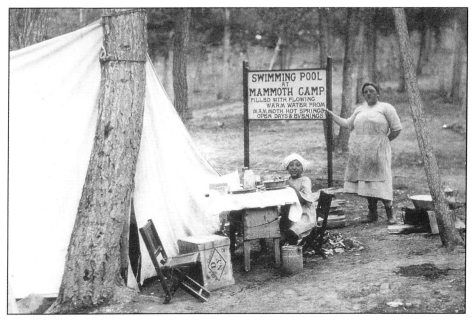

27. INSTITUTIONALIZED SWIMMING IN THE HOT SPRINGS. Swimming or soaking in the water from the Mammoth Hot Springs was sanctioned as a standard tourist activity in the 1920s. Park concessioners were allowed to set up bath houses and charge tourists to bathe in the hot spring waters, which had been diverted from the formation to their facilities. This particular scene is from the Mammoth Campground in 1922, courtesy of the National Park Service, Yellowstone National Park.

28. HAMILTON POOL AT OLD FAITHFUL. F. J. Haynes photographed the privately owned and operated swimming pool in the Old Faithful area. Courtesy of the Haynes Foundation Collection, Montana Historical Society.

29. FISHING CONE. William Henry Holmes's sketch of "The Fish-Pot" appeared in Hayden's *Twelfth Annual Report*. This very popular sketch was included in many guidebooks, picture books, and privately published books, especially in books written by individuals who had never actually toured the park or this part of Yellowstone Lake.

30. FISHING CONE. F. J. Haynes's photograph of individuals fishing from Fishing Cone. Courtesy of the Haynes Foundation Collection, Montana Historical Society.

31. Winter in Yellowstone. A lone figure in snowshoes stands at the edge of the Grand Canyon facing the Lower Falls. Courtesy of the Haynes Foundation Collection, Montana Historical Society.

32. Corkscrew Bridge. A corkscrew bridge at Sylvan Pass on the road between the East Entrance and the main road near Yellowstone Lake Hotel. Photograph by Engineer, Department of War, courtesy of the National Park Service, Yellowstone National Park.

time, the experience of the whole park, "the totality of experience" Joseph Sax describes for all national parks, is looked upon with affection and familiarity.[6]

Too often in our attempts to describe, criticize, or manage Yellowstone as a national park, we focus on the awe-inspiring side of Yellowstone's personality. Such attention is important. It is vital that views of Yellowstone's Grand Canyon are not obstructed by buildings or obscured by air pollution and haze. It is important that grizzlies live unfenced and untamed in the Yellowstone wilderness. It is necessary for Yellowstone as a national park to be managed in such a way that its integrity as a natural ecosystem is restored and maintained in the face of the park's popularity, politics, and economics. However, we are in no immediate danger of losing the awe-inspiring experiences that Yellowstone National Park provides. The park's spectacular and strange features will always attract and intrigue a devoted constituency that will act as watchdog to protect these necessary elements of the park experience. It is the character of the park, however, that we may be in danger of losing.

WINTER

Until recently, winter has been Yellowstone's off-season. "The place is deserted by all save the keepers at the hotels and the wild animals who make the Park their home."[7] One park historian suggests that winter has traditionally been a time for the park to heal or rejuvenate from the short but intense impact of summer tourism.[8] And, until recently, such a vision may have been valid. Before the advent of motorized snow-vehicles—snow coaches and snowmobiles, for example—only the hardy few who were willing to accept the realities of Yellowstone's extreme and harsh conditions visited the park during the winter. Most came on skis or snowshoes, made camp in the snow, and traveled in silence (photograph 31). These nomads found the park empty, quiet, and cold. Almost a century ago, a young private in the army stationed in Yellowstone on winter duty wrote in a letter to his sister saying, "Everything is so quiet that one can almost hear the solitude."[9] More recently, a winter visitor wrote, "I was alone with my thoughts. I felt a part of something. Infinity? Creation? How can I explain it? This was something I had to feel alone."[10] Over the past decade, Yellowstone has seen a rapid increase in winter use from under 7,000 to over 140,000 winter visitors.[11] Most of these tourists travel through the park on snowmobiles. And, not only has the number of visitors increased, but there has been an accompanying increase in winter services and facilities available to them.

Modern winter tourists are not as self-sufficient as were those of the past. They come on snowmobiles, stay in hotels, eat in restaurants, and refuel their vehicles at gas stations. Park concessioners have been hesitant to extend services into the winter season, but the NPS—goaded by special interest groups involved in providing tourist services outside the park—continues to propose that more winter support facilities be built or be made available inside the park. Such a situation is not unique to Yellowstone. "Many wildlands have thus experienced a progressive shift from values focused on a natural environment to more socially-oriented, facility dependent values."[12]

Many scientists argue that the ecological impact of snowmobiles is minimal, since so much of the park is protected deep beneath several feet of shielding snow. From a humanistic and historical perspective, however, the impact of a busy winter season is great. Traditionally, winter travel to and through Yellowstone has been slow, deliberate, and quiet, taking place in a landscape mostly devoid of humans and their trappings. Now, those who come to the park expecting solitude and silence find themselves instead among ever-increasing crowds and the roar of snowmobiles. Yellowstone's sense of place has withstood many assaults, modernizations, and changes, and in many ways, such improvements have served to make the park's spirit more meaningful and approachable. It is hard to believe, however, that the blue-gray exhaust haze and silence-shattering roar of snowmobiles—both of which linger long after the snowmobile has passed—should be allowed to force its way into the park's sense of place. The effects of large-scale snowmobile traffic will not form a new dimension to Yellowstone's sense of place so much as detract from or destroy a part of it. Eighty years ago when the first automobiles rolled into the park, the American public was not in a position to question whether this addition was appropriate. A similar decision faces us today. Snowmobiles—for all the fun, speed, and accessibility they provide—are not, as yet, part of Yellowstone's winter tradition. Surely there are more appropriate places for such a recreational activity.

Furthermore, it is not only winter travel which has traditionally required effort and sacrifice on the part of Yellowstone visitors. For the first fifty or sixty years of the park's existence, tourists expected a tour of Yellowstone to require some sacrifice. A persistent theme that reverberates through the park literature is that experiencing Yellowstone is "worth the effort" of the arduous journey. Before rudimentary roads were built, those who wished to see Yellowstone had to make their way through the park's thick stands of lodgepole pine:

> It is no easy undertaking to get here. A person must be in perfect health and strength to endure the horseback-ride over this mountain trail. I have seen some campaigning over what was called a rough country, but I must confess that I had no conception of what was involved in two hundred and fifty miles on horseback with a pack-train over the Yellowstone trail. Those weary miles, through dense thickets and over fallen timber . . . where one's eyes grow tired in looking for open spaces to crowd through; those miles of narrow trail up and down steep mountains and along the sides of cañons, where chasms yawn hundreds of feet beneath you . . . all have to be retraced on our return. But if it were ten times as long and ten times as difficult and dangerous, one sight of Old Faithful in full play, as we witnessed it to-night, and one view of this valley to the north, as I can see it now, would amply repay any one for all the difficulties to be encountered.[13]

Many early tourists included descriptions of the log-strewn forests through which they had to alternately ride, walk, and scramble. Others encouraged those who read their accounts to learn how to tie a "diamond hitch" before heading into Yellowstone. The diamond hitch was thought to be one of the few knots that effectively secured camping gear to cantankerous pack mules. Hence, the idea that seeing the park requires some effort, whether that effort is a sacrifice of time, money, or comfort, has long been part of the Yellowstone experience.

By making Yellowstone not only accessible but also easily accessible in summer and winter, the experience can become trivialized and its impact reduced. Olin Wheeler chastised those tourists who believed a visit to Yellowstone could be undertaken easily and without effort:

> I have known of tourists, both men and women, who seemed to think that there was to be no effort required on their part to see anything: that the geysers were to be brought to them on a server; that as they sat in the coaches the falls would change position so they could be viewed without leaving their seats; that nature had provided vast deposits of asphalt, so lo! a fine asphalt pavement was spread throughout the Park. Such tourists will suffer disappointment and deserve to. While there is no hardship, there

will be some fatigue. . . . As a matter of fact, when one has decided to visit the Park, practice in pedestrianism should be regularly indulged every day for a week or ten days prior to departure from home.[14]

Recently, a park ranger commented on the new type of winter visitor, one dependent upon the snowmobile:

I must wonder why they need a national park for what they do, and why a national park must spend so much money to enable them to do it. . . . But still, after all the justifications and rationalizing, the [snowmobiles] still don't quite fit. It's more than a physical squeeze; they simply aren't what we have in mind for Yellowstone. It's arrogant, but we're suspicious, and I think rightly so, of all that luxury and appliance when the park is supposed to be offering simpler joys . . . the rustic element of the park experience is too far along, and too well proven, to be so lightly compromised.[15]

In order to accommodate the needs of anticipated future winter crowds, the Park Service is initiating projects now to deal with their eventual arrival. A point that seems to have been overlooked, however, is that if support facilities do not exist, perhaps future crowds will not come. If there are no warming huts, no hotels, and no restaurants open in the winter, those who are unwilling to face Yellowstone on its own terms may stay away, and the traditional solitude, silence, and emptiness of a Yellowstone winter may be preserved. By making Yellowstone easily accessible in all seasons, by removing all obstacles to travel—snow, cold, lack of lodging, food, and transportation except for that provided by the individual—park managers will succeed in making common what is now uncommon. Yellowstone in winter will be like any other place, and that which is unique about a Yellowstone winter—its character—will disappear.

SETTING THE BOUNDARIES OF CARE AND CONCERN

The National Park Service's commitment to preserving the integrity of Yellowstone's sense of place should include preserving those parts of Yellowstone's historical and perceptual landscape that lie outside the park's physical, legal boundaries. Typically, experiencing Yellowstone does not begin the instant one crosses the park boundary. Instead, it is a journey that often begins miles or hundreds of miles from the park itself and years in advance of the actual visit. Such large measures of time and space are, naturally, outside the purview of the National Park Service. However, the NPS should be able to regulate, at least to some degree, the status of lands bordering the park. Prominent landmarks, landforms, and even roadways could be considered part and parcel of the Yellowstone experience, if the park's historical record and sense of place are used as criteria for the park's perceptual rather than political boundaries.

Paradise Valley and Emigrant Peak

Most guidebook authors—especially those associated with the Northern Pacific Railway whose spur line bisected the area—and a majority of the park's early tourists included in their Yellowstone accounts descriptions of Paradise Valley, the lovely, gently rolling, open valley of the lower Yellowstone River between the park's north entrance and Livingston, Montana. The valley was never prized as a nature preserve, since its fertile and easily irrigated soils and milder climate had already attracted settlement at the time of the park's creation. The mountains that enclose the valley, however, have caused many Yellowstone-bound travelers to pause. Emigrant Peak and Emigrant Gulch—named for large numbers of prospectors who were lured to this highest peak in the Snowy Mountains in search of gold in the mid-1800s—stand out on the landscape and in the park's written record. In his lecture tours, Langford recreated for his audience the experience of watching a mountain storm on Emigrant Peak:

> An exhibition of mountain phenomena, common in Montana greeted our eyes as we passed the Pyramid. A black cloud enveloped its summit casting its gloomy shadow over the adjacent peaks, and burst into a grand storm of more than an hour's duration when the vapors slowly receded, and the mountain emerged from them, bathed in a glow of sunlight. The magnificent changes in mountain scenery, occasioned by light and shade, during one of these terrific tempests, with all the incidental accompaniments of thunder, lightning, rain, snow and hail, must be seen to be appreciated.[16]

Ferdinand Hayden was awed by the peak's beauty, geology, and the magnificent views afforded by its heights, but in addition he recognized the importance of the whole mountain range as a source of water for the surrounding region: "This range . . . forms the great watershed between two portions of the Yellowstone River . . . and gives origin to some of the most important branches of that river. Large numbers of springs and small streams flow down from the mountains into the Yellowstone on the southwest side . . . the Big Bowlder, Rosebud, Clark's Fork, and Pryor's Fork, with their numerous branches."[17]

Local, small-scale farms, gold mines, and tourist facilities—all established over a century ago when placer mining was the dominant activity in the area—have always been a part of the Paradise Valley–Emigrant region's history. The openness, emptiness, and pastoral beauty of the valley and its mountains have impressed both those passing through and those embracing the isolation and making the area their home. However, as the modern world rediscovers the wonders of the Yellowstone area, nontraditional interests such as residential subdivisions—mainly for retirement or second homes—and large-scale tourism has begun to claim more and more of the public and private lands in Paradise Valley and the slopes of Emigrant Peak. It may be wise for local and federal planners to plan now for the sort of future they envision for this gateway corridor to Yellowstone National Park. Certainly, the whole valley cannot be annexed to the park, nor should it be, but the austere wildness of Emigrant Peak and the gardenlike or middle landscape of Paradise Valley should be recognized and evaluated in terms of their value as "place" and "habitat" as well as their historic significance as a route of passage into Yellowstone.

Cody Road

A very different landscape greets those who enter Yellowstone from the east. Rather than the green, bucolic fields of Paradise Valley, the fifty-three-mile stretch from Cody, Wyoming, to Yellowstone's East Gate is a drier, more rugged landscape filled with fantastically shaped rocks and the North Fork of the Shoshone River. Most of the land between Cody and Yellowstone National Park is contained within the Shoshone National Forest, the country's oldest national forest. To many, Shoshone National Forest belongs to Yellowstone. Its early establishment mirrors the concern that created Yellowstone as a national preserve: the idea that these unique and valuable regions should be publicly rather than privately owned. From a humanistic perspective, the Shoshone lands and natural features—rock and river—are both part of the Yellowstone experience and part of the Yellowstone ecosystem.

"The Cody Road"—or, as the Lions Club of Cody would have us believe, the "most scenic seventy miles in the world"—connects Cody with Yellow-stone's east entrance.[18] At first, the steep grades through the Absaroka Mountains that border Yellowstone to the east posed a formidable obstacle to tourists and a formidable puzzle to civil engineers. Hence, although construction began on the road in 1890, it was not opened until 1903. At the time of the Cody Road's construction, automobiles were not yet allowed in the park. For that reason, "corkscrew bridges" were built (photograph 32). These spiraling structures were a means by which horse-drawn carriages could conquer the steep grades of Sylvan Pass. One park employee known for his "truthful lies" described a corkscrew bridge as so crooked and twisted that "you pass one place three times before you get by it, and then meet yourself on the road coming back."[19] Most of the park's corkscrew bridges have now been removed and replaced with modern bridges. Others were left by the wayside to rot as modern, macadamized roads were laid nearby on slopes graded for automobile traffic. Like the stagecoaches, beggar bears, and silent winters, corkscrew bridges are quickly passing from the public's memory of an earlier Yellowstone experience.

Despite its precipitous ascents and descents and thanks to the engineering feat of the corkscrew bridge, the Cody Road quickly became a popular route by which tourists entered Yellowstone, especially for Wyoming residents and those who were traveling in their own conveyances rather than by rail. Most tourists stopped in Cody for supplies—as many do today—and it was at this point that their Yellowstone adventure began:

> Wednesday morning we started on for the Park which, we were told, was still sixty four miles distant. We were now approaching the mountains and had passed through some gorgeous scenery. The road was lined with travelers in wagons, in carriages, in coaches and on horseback, going to and from the Park. . . . Our road led us up the North Fork, the scenery of which thrilled us to the toes after our three week's sight seeing of sage brush and sandy wastes.[20]

For those traveling into the park from Cody, the changes in the land prompted a change in attitude, and in most people's minds, the Cody Road belongs to its destination—Yellowstone—more so than its departure city.

If Yellowstone tourist guidebooks are any indication of what is typically included in a Yellowstone Park tour, the Shoshone is yet another of Yellow-stone's treasures. The *Haynes Guide* and other contemporary guidebooks encouraged sightseers to find various shapes expertly carved by wind and water in the walls of the North Fork canyon—among them the Holy City, the Wooden Shoe, Ptarmigan Mountain, Thor's Anvil, and the Mutilated Hand.[21] And, members of the local Lion's Club added other caricatures to the list—the Laughing Pig, the Bear, and the Goose, as well as the Old Fashioned Lady, the Devil's Elbow, the Playground of the Gods, and the Garden of the Goops. For this and other reasons, the Northern Pacific Railroad considered the Cody Road through the Shoshone National Forest "a regular and spectacular part of the trip" to Yellowstone: "To visit Yellowstone without seeing the Cody Road is comparable to going all the way to New York and then coming away without seeing Broadway or Fifth Avenue. It is the 'show road' to or from the Park."[22]

The ambiguity of Yellowstone's perceptual eastern border is obvious in the various attempts to define the actual distance of the Cody Road. In most cases, the distinction between the Shoshone region and the park's official boundary is blurred. Most individuals and organizations assume that the Cody Road extends from Cody, Wyoming, all the way to the main highway inside the park. On the map, it is fifty-three miles from Cody to the park's eastern border and twenty-seven miles from the border to the junction with Yellowstone's grand loop road. Hence, the entire distance—or much of it—from Cody to Yellowstone is, at least locally, considered part of the park.

In recent years, residents of the Shoshone region along with concerned individuals from across the United States and around the world worked together to have the North Fork of the Shoshone River designated as wild and scenic. Such status secures the river's "naturalness" by severely restricting future development or use of the stream and its environs and solidifies the North Fork's image as a natural feature worth preserving for its own sake as well as that of public rather than private interests. Hence, in the public's mind, as well as in the eyes of the law, the corridor along the Cody Road through the Shoshone National Forest and into Yellowstone National Park is a part of the larger region of concern known as Yellowstone.

Devil's Slide

The Devil's Slide—one of Yellowstone's classic, natural wonders—actually lies outside the park's northern boundary. However, in Yellowstone's historic record, the Devil's Slide figures prominently as part of the park experience (see photograph 10). In his discovery account, Langford assumed the

Devil's Slide was part of Yellowstone: "In future years, when the wonders of the Yellowstone are incorporated into the family of fashionable resorts, there will be few of its attractions surpassing in interest this marvelous freak of the elements."[23] And, as predicted, future tourists did see the odd, geologic feature as their first taste of the many wonders to follow over the course of a park tour. The sudden appearance of the slide around a bend in the Yellowstone River still initiates the park visitor to the strange and intriguing land lying just ahead.

However, despite the fact that most people assume that the Devil's Slide lies within the legal boundaries of the park and enjoys the same protection as other park features, the Devil's Slide is on private property. It belongs to the Church Universal and Triumphant (CUT), a religious sect with headquarters on the park's northern border. The slide is not accessible to the general public, although one can view the massive feature in its entirety from a vantage point along the highway across the Yellowstone River. The land upon which the slide is situated has been fenced off with barbed wire to contain the cattle that graze on surrounding CUT lands. If the National Park Service had been aware of the Devil's Slide's importance to park history, stronger attempts might have been made to secure funds for the slide's purchase in 1980 when owner Malcolm Forbes—after attempting to sell it to the U.S. Forest Service—sold it to the CUT. However, history and tradition are often overlooked or discounted when economic and political forces are called into play, and the Devil's Slide—through an inattention to tradition—was allowed to slip out of the hands of Yellowstone managers.

Grasshopper Glacier

Grasshopper Glacier is another feature that, although "it lies just outside the limits of the Park proper, it is, notwithstanding, part and parcel of the wonders of the Park region."[24] Grasshopper Glacier, so-named because of the number of grasshoppers that are visible, frozen in the glacier's ice, is not located adjacent to the park but lies in the Beartooth Wilderness Area in the Absaroka Mountains northeast of the park. Descriptions of the glacier are included in the Yellowstone *Haynes Guide*: "The Grasshopper Glacier! This extraordinary natural phenomenon just across the park line, fits well in the scheme of the great wonderland."[25]

In no danger of development or exclusion, Grasshopper Glacier is introduced here merely as an example of how ill-defined and subjective are the perceptual boundaries delineating the Yellowstone. It is no wonder, then, that the various groups voicing concern over their interests in the "Greater Yellowstone" have as many different mental maps and agendas as to what comprises the Greater Yellowstone as they have proposals for its management. The park's history can provide valuable and viable evidence for these various groups to support or disprove different claims as to what has been traditionally considered a part of the park and the park experience.

PRESERVING CHARACTER

In 1904, the McLaughlin family traveled to Yellowstone National Park by horse and buggy. Forty years later, after visiting the park again, Carrie Todd McLaughlin—wife and mother of the clan—recorded their experiences "in order to preserve these notes in permanent form and in sufficient number to permit each one interested to have a copy":

> We . . . went over the same route, this time by automobile, covering in three days the mileage that before had required five weeks. In the Park we found but little change; cabins had replaced the camping facilities, and the number of tourists had multiplied many fold; some of the geysers had ceased to flow, while others had broken out. But the Black Growler still growls as fiercely; Old Faithful still throws up every sixty three minutes; the colors of the cañon are as vivid; the cataracts are as awe-inspiring and the odor of sulphur pervading the atmosphere is still as overpowering.[26]

In the one-and-a-quarter centuries since its establishment, Yellowstone has matured, certainly, but in many ways it has not changed. The sense of place experienced by millions of park visitors has persisted over the course of the park's dramatic history. However, the management emphasis now placed on science, economics, and ecological restoration may desensitize the park's public and keep it from experiencing both the personality and character of the park. If park managers do not come to recognize and defend Yellowstone's character, its spirit of place, future generations of park visitors may find that the Yellowstone experience has become a generic vacation resort in a con-trived wilderness setting. Scientific management based on some ambiguous state of ecological health or fitness cannot predict public opinion, nor can science explain people's attraction to and affection for the parks. Science and ecological standards are and should always be important tools in the management of any natural area, but science alone cannot and should not inject values into the decision-making process. An understanding of a park's history is at least as important, if not more so, than is an understanding of its present role as an example of wild nature or an intact ecosystem. "National parks do have scientific purposes," writes Tom Vale, geographer and historian of the national parks. Parks "represent the best opportunity to protect nature in the world." But they do more. National parks "have humanistic purposes as well, such as exploring our pasts, expanding our knowledge, stretching our muscles, inspiring our emotions, renewing our psyches, and encouraging economics."[27] Yellowstone is a place for all these activities, but it is also valuable in and of itself.

A humanistic perspective toward park management has implications for the other national parks administered by the NPS, especially those few truly wild landscapes within the national park system. The sense of place associated with Alaskan national parks, for example, conjures up images of inaccessible, pristine, austere environments. If Yellowstone National Park is representative of an ideal national park wilderness and can accommodate upwards of three million visitors over the course of a summer, what does this purport for the future of Denali, Gates of the Arctic, and Wrangell–St. Elias National Parks?

Recognizing national parks as entities rather than potential ideals may save some parks from *becoming* humanized. This perspective allows an appreciation for the constraints and opportunities that should be intrinsically a part of every park's management program. Hence, achieving "the national park ideal" becomes a task of balancing change and permanence, science and history, in the national parks *individually* rather than collectively. This sort of management philosophy requires that we discard the notion of Yellowstone National Park as "the ideal" national park and hence as a model for management practices in all nature parks. The importance of Yellowstone's establishment as a milestone in the nature protection movement cannot and should not be denied. However, we should begin to move our thinking away from the notion that Yellowstone epitomizes what a national park should be. Other parks have equally important, albeit different, histories and personalities and are "places" in their own right. Their designations as national parks represent other, equally valid points on the continuum of our evolving appreciation for nature. These parks should be managed so as to emphasize their individual qualities and characteristics—their spirits of place—rather than attempting to emulate Yellowstone's. Evolution is a continuum. However, "in any continuum, some points are always more interesting than others."[28] For many of us, Yellowstone National Park will always be more interesting than other parks not because it is the world's first national park but because of its enduring and endearing spirit of place.

FUTURE OF THE PLACE

There is much yet to be learned about Yellowstone. So too is there much yet to be learned about each of the national parks and our relationship to them—as natural landscapes and as places. Models explaining biological evolution can go only so far as a framework for our understanding cultural evolution. Biological evolution differs from cultural evolution in that people can actively and purposefully alter the course of cultural change. Not only can we give meanings to the world around us and thereby create places, but we also have the power to control the forces of our own making—economic constraints, political agendas, and scientific and technological capabilities. We can make decisions that will ensure a future for Yellowstone—and all other parks and places that are important to us, from the nearness of our own backyards to the vastness of Antarctica—that are in keeping with both the history of, and our hopes for, the strong and vital spirits of these places. In the national parks, especially, we need to be aware of the limits we set for ourselves when we insist that they be representative of nature. We all know that our attitudes toward nature change over time, but should our attitudes toward individual national parks change as well?

In this work, an attempt was made to bring part of Yellowstone National Park's past—and thereby its present—to light by suggesting that there are different ways or perspectives from which to interpret the park's written record. The perspective introduced here focuses on Yellowstone's history as place, as a shared geographic and cultural reality, and its powerful and persistent spirit of place. Such a study reveals the strong ties that bind—and have bound—people to this place. It suggests that Yellowstone's spirit is not immutable; nor is it capricious, undisciplined, and uncontrolled. Instead, the sense of place people experience here has blossomed from a simple beginning, full of potential, to a widely recognized, complex, and controversial place richly endowed with meanings. Patterns of continuity are at least as strong as patterns of change, so there is hope that future generations can come to know the same Yellowstone that touched past generations.

In this work, too, an attempt was made to show that a clear and complete understanding of a national park or any historic, public place must include an understanding of the original conditions that initiated its evolution. By accepting Yellowstone's past as an inseparable part of its present rather than as an obsolete and transitional stage, park managers and decision makers may be able, yet, to preserve and protect what is best about the park—its spirit of place.

NOTES

INTRODUCTION

1. Lewis R. Freeman, *Down the Yellowstone* (London: William Heinemann Ltd, 1923), 29–30.
2. Wallace Stegner, "The Marks of Human Passage," in *Mirror of America*, ed. David Harmon (Boulder, Colo.: Roberts Rinehart, Inc., 1989), 169.
3. Dorr G. Yeager, *Your Western National Parks* (New York: Dodd, Mead and Company, 1947), 53.

CHAPTER 1

1. At the time of Yellowstone's establishment as a national park, much of what is now Yosemite National Park had already been set aside by the federal government as a state park. Hence, much of the reverence for Yellowstone as the place where the federal government first withdrew land from the public domain to be used as a public park is misplaced. However, the Yosemite Park Act of 1864 called for Yosemite to be administered by the state of California rather than the federal government, whereas Yellowstone National Park managers answered to Washington. Several wonderful books deal both specifically and broadly with the historical and political intricacies and motivation behind Yellowstone's creation as a national park. Among them are the following: Hans Huth, *Nature and the American* (Berkeley: University of California Press, 1957); Roderick Nash, *Wilderness and the American Mind* (New Haven, Conn.: Yale University Press, 1975); Aubrey L. Haines, *The Yellowstone Story*, 2 vols. (Boulder: Colorado Associated Press, 1977); Alfred Runte, *National Parks: The American Experience* (Lincoln: University of Nebraska Press, 1979) and the second, revised edition of 1987, and *Yosemite: The Embattled Wilderness* (Lincoln: University of Nebraska Press, 1990); John F. Sears, *Sacred Places: American Tourist Attractions in the Nineteenth Century* (New York: Oxford University Press, 1989); Chris J. Majoc, *The Selling of Wonderland* (Doctoral diss., University of New Mexico, 1992).
2. Runte, *National Parks*, 2d ed., 1.
3. W. Turrentine Jackson, "The Creation of Yellowstone National Park," *Missis-*

sippi Valley Historical Review 29 (1943): 187–88. The use of the term "evolution" to describe national park evolution can also be found in the following texts: Huth, *Nature and the American*; William C. Everhart, *The National Park Service* (New York: Praeger Publishers, 1972); Edward Abbey, *Desert Solitaire* (New York: Ballantine Books, 1979); Ronald A. Foresta, *America's National Parks and Their Keepers* (Washington, D.C.: Resources for the Future, 1984).

4. Paul Shepard in Linda Graber, *Wilderness as Sacred Space* (Washington, D.C.: Association of American Geographers, 1976), 69.

5. Foresta, *America's National Parks*, 1.

6. See Stephen Jay Gould, "Opus 2000," *Natural History* 100, no. 8 (August 1991):12–18.

7. See especially Everhart, *National Park Service*; Foresta, *America's National Parks*; John Ise, *Our National Park Policy* (Baltimore: Johns Hopkins University Press, 1985); and Horace M. Albright, *The Birth of the National Park Service* (Salt Lake City: Howe Brothers, 1985).

8. Foresta in *America's National Parks*, for example, recognizes three political or administrative eras: the Mather-Albright era (1891–1920s), the Roosevelt-Kennedy era (1930s–1960s), and the modern era (1960s to present). Runte in *National Parks* is less exacting in his time spans but divides the history of the national parks into eras defined by public motivation for creating parks.

9. Robert Barbee and Paul Schullery, "Yellowstone: After the Smoke Clears," *National Parks* 63, no. 3–4 (March/April 1989):18.

10. For the most comprehensive bibliography of historical documents pertaining to Yellowstone National Park, see Lee H. Whittlesey, *Wonderland Nomenclature: A History of the Place Names of Yellowstone National Park* (Helena: Montana Historical Society Press, 1988).

11. See Haines, *Yellowstone Story* in two volumes; Richard A. Bartlett, *Yellowstone: A Wilderness Besieged* (Tucson: University of Arizona Press, 1985); and Alston Chase, *Playing God in Yellowstone* (Boston: Atlantic Monthly Press, 1986).

12. See Albright, *Birth*; Chase, *Playing God*; and Majoc, *The Selling of Wonderland*.

13. In tabulating results, the accounts were divided into six time periods: 1870–1879, 1880–1889, 1890–1899, 1900–1914, 1915–1929, and 1930–1991. Sampling was biased heavily toward the early decades of the park's history, since this was a formative period that set the stage for much of what was to follow. Each time period contains approximately fifty accounts. In order to compare the park's sense of place before and after the introduction of the private automobile in 1915 and before and after the establishment of the National Park Service in 1916, another division was set at 1914–1915. The largest time period, between 1930 and 1991, includes the same number of accounts as earlier, smaller periods because fewer descriptions of the park experience appear in this latter period, although more has been written about Yellowstone National Park in the last three decades than in the preceding century. Modern

Yellowstone accounts and publications are more typically highly illustrated newspaper or magazine articles that focus on some current issue—wildlife management, local, regional, or federal politics, or the perils or pleasures of tourism, for example. Or, they are anthologies containing excerpts from earlier works accompanied by both historical and modern photographs or other illustrations. Certainly, too, the scientific and academic press has published much in recent decades on various aspects of Yellowstone's physical and human environment, and many of these materials were included in this analysis. However, such works rarely provide an insight into the particular author's affective response to the park as place. It might be said that although more and more people are both visiting and writing about Yellowstone, fewer and fewer are recording a sense of the place. Whether this is a result of the loss or weakening of Yellowstone's spirit of place or the result of modern tourists' failure to allow themselves to experience the place remains to be seen.

14. A complete list of sources is included in the bibliography.

15. In John Sears's *Sacred Places*, he, too, found that "no obvious differences stood out in the literature by male and female authors." Sears goes on to point out that "tourism, unlike hunting or plowing, tending a flower garden or caring for children, was never gender identified. Both men and women participated in it, often together, sometimes with children, and in doing so shared the same space" (Sears, *Sacred Places*, 8).

16. A. C. Peale in Ferdinand V. Hayden, *Sixth Annual Report of the United States Geological Survey of the Territories* (Washington, D.C.: GPO, 1873), 160.

17. Descriptions of the nature of the sublime can be found in Marjorie Hope Nicolson, *Mountain Gloom and Mountain Glory* (Ithaca: Cornell University Press, 1959); Denis Cosgrove, *Social Formation and Symbolic Landscape* (London: Croom Helm, 1984); and, as the source for the characteristics of the sublime as described here, Elizabeth McKinsey, *Niagara Falls: Icon of the American Sublime* (New York: Cambridge University Press, 1985).

18. Marshall in Robert E. Strahorn, *To the Rockies and Beyond* (Chicago: Belford, Clarke and Company, 1881), 212.

19. A. M. Mattoon, "The Yellowstone National Park, Summer of 1889," Handwritten journal (Yellowstone Park Research Library, Mammoth Hot Springs, Wyo., 1917), 99.

20. Cornelius Hedges, "Journal of Judge Cornelius Hedges," *Contributions to the Historical Society of Montana* 5 (1904): 378.

21. Edwin J. Stanley, *Rambles in Wonderland* (New York: D. Appleton and Company, 1880), 60.

22. Earl of Dunraven, *The Great Divide* (London: Chatto and Windus, 1876), 331.

23. William M. Thayer, *Marvels of the New West* (Norwich, Conn.: The Henry Bill Publishing Company, 1888), 82.

24. Rose Lambert Price, *A Summer in the Rockies* (London: Sampson Low, Marston and Company, Ltd., 1898), 180.

25. Alma White, *With God in the Yellowstone* (Zaraphath, N.J.: Pillar of Fire, 1933), 53.

26. Cal C. Clawson, "The Region of the Wonderful Lake—Yellowstone," *New Northwest* (Deer Lodge, Mont.), 18 May 1872, 20.

27. Thompson P. McElrath, *The Yellowstone Valley* (St. Paul: Pioneer Press, 1880), 99.

28. Clawson, "Region," 2.

29. Olin D. Wheeler, *Wonderland '97* (St. Paul: Northern Pacific Railway, 1897), 43.

30. W. C. Riley, *Official Guide to the Yellowstone National Park* (St. Paul: W.C. Riley, 1889), 72–73.

31. George W. Wingate, *Through the Yellowstone Park on Horseback* (New York: O. Judd Company, 1886), 88–89.

32. Almon Gunnison, *Rambles Overland* (Boston: Universalist Publishing House, 1884), 49.

33. Marie M. Augspurger, *Yellowstone National Park* (Middletown, Ohio: The Naegele-Auer Printing Company, 1948), 1.

34. James C. Fennell, "In the Yellowstone Park," *California Illustrated* 2, no. 3 (1892): 362–63.

35. Otto Zardetti, *Westlich! oder Durch den fernen Westen Nord-Amerikas* (Mainz: Verlag von Franz Kirchheim, 1887), 49.

36. Ferdinand V. Hayden, "The Wonders of the West—II," *Scribner's Monthly* 3, no. 4 (1872): 389.

37. Ferdinand V. Hayden, *Preliminary Report of the U.S. Geological Survey of Montana and Portions of Adjacent Territories; being a Fifth Annual Report of Progress* (Washington, D.C.: GPO, 1872), 76.

38. Union Pacific System, *Geyserland* (Omaha: W.H. Murray, 1923), 13.

39. Theodore Gerrish, *Life in the World's Wonderland* (Biddleford, Maine: Privately published, 1886), 194.

40. Northern Pacific Railway, *The Way to Wonderland: Yellowstone National Park* (St. Paul: Northern Pacific Railway, 1935), 25.

41. J. E. Williams, "Vacation Notes: Summer of 1888: Through the Yellowstone Park," *Amherst (Mass.) Record* (1888), 12.

42. James Richardson, *Wonders of the Yellowstone Region* (London: Blackie and Son, Paternoster Buildings, E.C, 1876), 2.

43. John H. Raftery, "Historical Sketch of Yellowstone National Park," *Annals of Wyoming* 15, no. 2 (1943): 125.

44. L. Gannett, *Sweet Land* (Garden City, N.Y.: Doubleday, Doran and Company, Inc., 1934), 171.

45. Paul Schullery, *Mountain Time* (New York: Simon and Schuster, 1988), 39.

46. Schullery, *Mountain Time*, 39.

47. Dunraven, *Great Divide*, 188.

48. Hiram M. Chittenden, *The Yellowstone National Park* (Cincinnati: R. Clarke Company, 1895), 189.

49. Ray S. Baker, "A Place of Marvels: Yellowstone Park As It Now Is," *Century Magazine* 66, no.4 (August 1903): 490.

50. Wallace Smith, *On the Trail in Yellowstone* (New York: Putnam's, 1924), 16–17.

51. William G. Robbins, "Triumphal Narratives and the Northern West," *Montana Magazine of Western History* 42, no. 2 (spring 1992): 64.

52. John L. Stoddard, *John L. Stoddard's Lectures*, vol. 10 (Boston: Balch Brothers Company, 1898), 208.

53. Runte, *National Parks*, 11.

54. Talmage in Charles H. Gates, *Yellowstone National Park, Alaska and the White Pass* (Toledo, Ohio: Franklin Printing and Engraving Company, 1903), 9.

55. Editors of *Scribner's Monthly*, "The Yellowstone National Park," *Scribner's Monthly* 4, no. 1 (May 1872): 121.

56. Gerrish, *World's Wonderland*, 216.

57. Stoddard, *Lectures*, 255–256.

58. Joe Chapple, *A' Top O' the World* (Boston: Chapple Publishing Company, Ltd., 1922), 10.

59. Wingate, *Through the Yellowstone*, 74–75.

60. Schullery, *Mountain Time*, 163.

61. Jim Carrier, *Letters from the Yellowstone* (Boulder, Colo.: Roberts Rinehart, Inc., 1987), 54–55.

62. Montana Department of Agriculture and Publicity, *Resources and Opportunities of Montana* (Helena: Independent Publishing Company, 1918), 104.

63. John Muir, *Our National Parks* (Madison: University of Wisconsin Press, 1981), 59.

64. Schullery, *Mountain Time*, 162.

65. Gustavus C. Doane in *Battle Drums and Geysers*, Orrin H. Bonney and Lorraine Bonney (Chicago: Swallow Press, Inc., 1970), 332.

66. Hayden, *Preliminary Report*, 162.

67. Schullery, *Mountain Time*, 169.

CHAPTER 2

1. For discussions of who was the first to enter the Yellowstone region, see Merrill J. Mattes, "Behind the Legend of Colter's Hell: The Early Exploration of Yellowstone National Park," *Mississippi Valley Historical Review* 36 (1949): 251–82; Haines, *Yellowstone Story*; Joel C. Janetski, *Indians of the Yellowstone Park* (Salt Lake City, Utah: Bonneville Books, 1987); and Fred R. Gowans, *A Fur Trade History of Yellowstone Park* (Orem, Utah: Mountain Grizzly Publications, 1989).

2. For information on the origin of place-names within the park, see Lee H. Whittlesey, *Yellowstone Place Names* (Helena: Montana Historical Society Press, 1988). For information on the park's current and past road systems, see Bob R. O'Brien, "The Future Road System of Yellowstone National Park," *Annals of the Association of American Geographers* 56, no. 3 (1966): 385–407.

3. Joseph Weixellman, "The Power to Evoke Wonder: Native Americans and the Geysers of Yellowstone National Park" (Masters thesis, Montana State University, 1992).

4. See especially Jackson, "Creation"; Huth, *Nature*; Bonney and Bonney, *Battle Drums*; Nash, *Wilderness*; Haines, *Yellowstone Story*; Ise, *Our National Park*; Runte, *National Parks* and *Yosemite*; Albright, *Birth*; Bartlett, *Wilderness Besieged*.

5. Yi-Fu Tuan, "Language and the Making of Place: A Narrative-Descriptive Approach," *Annals of the Association of American Geographers* 81, no. 4 (1991): 684–96.

6. See N. P. Langford in David E. Folsom, "The Folsom-Cook Exploration of the Upper Yellowstone in the Year 1869," *Contributions to the Historical Society of Montana* 5 (1904): 348–69; Jackson, "Creation"; Aubrey Haines in Charles W. Cook, David E. Folsom, and William Peterson, *The Valley of the Upper Yellowstone* (Norman: University of Oklahoma Press, 1965); Bonney and Bonney, *Battle Drums*; Joe B. Frantz, "The Meaning of Yellowstone," *Montana Magazine of Western History* 22, no. 3 (July 1972): 5–11; Haines, *Yellowstone Story*; Bartlett, *Wilderness Besieged*.

7. Haines, *Yellowstone Story*, 84.

8. Haines, *Yellowstone Story*, 101.

9. Lee Whittlesey has reprinted and annotated the original *Scribner's Monthly* article in his *Lost in the Yellowstone: Truman Everts's "37 Days of Peril"* (Salt Lake City: University of Utah Press, 1995).

10. It could be argued that several other articles and lecture notes written by members of the Washburn-Langford-Doane expeditions should be considered when discussing "discovery accounts," and I include them here for purposes of historical accuracy and thoroughness. However, the following accounts—either in their original published form or as sources for other authors' descriptions of Yellowstone—were not published as early as the discovery accounts nor did they reach as wide an audience. They have therefore not been included in the list of discovery accounts. These auxiliary accounts include the following: (1) Cornelius Hedges's "Journal of Judge Cornelius Hedges" in *Contributions to the Historical Society of Montana* of 1904, five newspaper accounts included in Louis C. Cramton's *Early History of the Yellowstone National Park and Its Relation to National Park Policies* of 1932 as well as an unpublished letter written to his sister on 11 October 1872; (2) Nathaniel Langford's "Manuscripts of Lectures Given by N. P. Langford during Winter of 1870–71," "The Yellowstone Expedition" in Louis Cramton's book cited above, and the *Diary of the Washburn Expedition to the Yellowstone and Firehole Rivers in the Year 1870* published by the F.J. Haynes Company in 1905; (3) General Henry D. Washburn's "The Yellowstone Expe-

dition" in *Mining Statistics West of the Rocky Mountains*, 42nd Cong., 1st Sess., House Ex. Doc. No. 10, SN-1470, 213–16, which was also reprinted in Louis Cramton's *Early History*; and (4) Walter Trumbull's "Yellowstone Papers No. One" and "Yellowstone Papers No. Two" in the *Rocky Mountain Daily Gazette* (Helena, Mont.) of 18 and 19 October 1870, and the "Yellowstone Papers" in the *Rocky Mountain Weekly Gazette* (Helena, Mont.) of 24 and 31 October 1870.

11. See John L. Allen, "An Analysis of the Exploratory Process," *Geographical Review* 66, no. 2 (1972): 13–39, and William H. Goetzmann and William N. Goetzmann, *The West of the Imagination* (New York: W.W. Norton, 1986).

12. For an excellent and comprehensive compilation of trapper-era documents, see Gowans, *Fur Trade History*.

13. N. P. Langford, "The Wonders of the Yellowstone, Part Two," *Scribner's Monthly* 2, no. 2 (June 1871): 113–29; see also Walter Trumbull, "The Washburn Yellowstone Expedition, Number Two," *Overland Monthly* 6, no. 6 (June 1871): 489–96.

14. Hayden, *Preliminary Report*, 79, 82, and 94–95, respectively.

15. Frances Fuller Victor, *The River of the West* (Oakland: Brooks-Sterling Company, 1974), 75. Whether Meek or another early Yellowstone visitor came up with the "Pittsburgh" analogy is debatable. Victor admits to using outside sources in reconstructing parts of Meek's life. It is likely that various articles in *The Montana Post*, a newspaper published in Virginia City, Montana, provided a good portion of Meek's supposed commentary on the Yellowstone region.

16. Hayden, *Preliminary Report*, 112.

17. Victor, *River*, 45–46.

18. Mattes, "Behind the Legend," 282.

19. Ferdinand von Hochstetter, *Neu = Seeland* (Stuttgart, Germany: Cotta'scher Verlag, 1863), 260.

20. Ferdinand von Hochstetter [translated] in Hayden, *Preliminary Report*, 176.

21. Hayden, *Preliminary Report*, 67 and 65; Hayden, "Wonders," 390.

22. Peale in Hayden, *Preliminary Report*, 174.

23. Peale in Ferdinand V. Hayden, *Sixth Annual Report of the United States Geological Survey of the Territories* (Washington, D.C.: GPO, 1873), 125.

24. N. P. Langford, "The Ascent of Mount Hayden," *Scribner's Monthly* 6, no. 2 (June 1873): 157.

25. Langford, "Wonders, Part Two," 128.

26. As originally published in German: "Wenn aber erst mit der fortschreitenden Colonisation von Neu = Seeland die Gegend zugänglicher wird, dann werden Tausende von Menschen . . . dahin pilgern, wo die Natur in der herrlichsten Gegend, im besten und mildesten Klima so merkwürdige Phänomene zeigt, und in so unerhörter Anzahl und Fülle die heilkraftigsten warmen Quellen geschaffen hat" (Hochstetter, *Neu = Seeland*, 36–37).

27. Hayden in Bonney and Bonney, *Battle Drums*, 422.

28. Gustavus C. Doane, "The Report of Lieutenant Gustavus C. Doane upon the So-called Yellowstone Expedition of 1870," Sen. Exec. Doc. No. 51, 41st Congress, 3rd Session (1871), 16.

29. Hayden, Preliminary Report, 92.

30. Langford, "Wonders, Part Two," 125.

31. Doane, "The Report," 31.

32. Henry D. Washburn in Bonney and Bonney, Battle Drums, 216.

33. Nicolson, Mountain Gloom, 1.

34. Folsom, "Exploration," 363.

35. McKinsey, Niagara Falls, 18.

36. Gunnison, Rambles Overland, 30–31.

37. N. P. Langford, "The Wonders of the Yellowstone, Part One," Scribner's Monthly 2, no. 1 (May 1871): 1–17 at 15.

38. Clawson, "Region," 14.

39. A. M. Cleland, Through Wonderland (Chicago: Rand McNally, 1910), 19.

40. R. E. Strahorn, Rockies and Beyond, 79.

41. E. F. Erk, A Merry Crusade to the Golden Gate (Akron, Ohio: Werner, 1906), 42; Carrie A. Strahorn, Fifteen Thousand Miles by Stage (New York: Putnam's, 1911), 419.

42. In Martyn J. Bowden's "The Invention of American Tradition", Journal of Historical Geography 18, no. 1(1992): 3–26, Bowden suggests that the transformation of terra incognita into geographical reality can be described as a series of distinct steps: image formation, myth creation, invented tradition, and universalization. Yellowstone's evolution as place—at first glance—does seem to follow such a pattern. However, deviations from the Bowden model throw light on the unique circumstances of Yellowstone's history.

43. See Carlos A. Schwantes, "Landscapes of Opportunity," Montana Magazine of Western History 43, no. 2 (spring 1993): 38–53.

44. J. H. Beadle, The Undeveloped West (Philadelphia: National Publishing Company, 1873), 678.

45. Robert E. Strahorn, The Enchanted Land (Omaha, Nebr.: New West Publishing Company, 1881), 31.

46. Williams, "Vacation Notes," 8.

47. W. W. Wylie, Yellowstone National Park (Kansas City, Mo.: Ramsey, Millett and Hudson, 1882), 1.

48. Flora Chase Pierce, Letter dated 8 August 1897 (Yellowstone Research Library, Mammoth Hot Springs, Wyo., 1897), n.p.

49. Margaret Andrews Cruikshank, "A Lady's Trip to Yellowstone in 1883: 'Earth Could Not Furnish Another Such Sight,' " in Montana Magazine of Western History 39, no. 1 (winter 1989): 11.

50. Cruikshank, "Lady's Trip," 4.

51. Wingate, *Through the Yellowstone*, 94.

52. Henry J. Winser, *The Great Northwest* (New York: G.P. Putnam's Sons, 1883), 31.

53. Edwards Roberts, *Shoshone and Other Western Wonders* (New York: Harper and Brothers, 1889), 234.

54. Stanley, *Rambles*, 98.

55. Edward Marston, *Frank's Ranche or My Holiday in the Rockies* (London: Sampson Low, Marston, Searle, and Rivington, 1886), 121–22.

56. Doane, "The Report," 282.

57. William E. Strong, *A Trip to the Yellowstone National Park in July, August, and September, 1875*, Richard A. Bartlett, ed. (Norman: University of Oklahoma Press, 1968), 49. Gustavus Doane accompanied General W. E. Strong's Yellowstone Expedition of 1875, so it is possible that Strong learned of the "sun being blocked out" directly from Doane rather than from Doane's published journal.

58. Gerrish, *World's Wonderland*, 224.

59. Dunnell in Hayden, *Preliminary Report*, xviii–xix.

60. Wingate, *Through the Yellowstone*, 11; italics mine.

61. Chittenden, *Yellowstone Park*, 209–10.

62. Olin D. Wheeler, *Wonderland 1906* (St. Paul: Northern Pacific Railway, 1906), 24.

CHAPTER 3

1. For example, the frozen cascade phrase appears in Richardson, *Yellowstone Region*; William C. Bryant, *Picturesque America*, 2 vols. (New York: D. Appleton and Company, 1872); Henry J. Norton, *Wonderland Illustrated* (Virginia City, Mont.: Harry J. Norton, 1873); Dunraven, *Great Divide*; Stanley, *Rambles*; R. E. Strahorn, *Enchanted Land*; L. P. Brockett, *Our Western Empire* (Philadelphia: Bradley and Company, 1881); and Winser, *Great Northwest*.

2. Archibald Geikie, *Geological Sketches at Home and Abroad* (New York: Macmillan, 1892), 222.

3. Philetus W. Norris, *Calumet of the Coteau* (Philadelphia: J.B. Lippincott and Company, 1884), 70.

4. Edward Pierrepont, *Fifth Avenue to Alaska* (New York: G.P. Putnam's Sons, 1884), 243.

5. H. Credner, "Der National-Park am Yellowstone," *Geographischer Zeitschrift* 1 (1895): 85.

6. Hayden, *Preliminary Report*, 70.

7. Hayden, *Preliminary Report*, 69.

8. Dunraven, *Great Divide*, 196.

9. Langford, "Wonders, Part One," 9.

10. Hayden, *Preliminary Report*, 78–79.

11. J. W. Clampitt, *Echoes from the Rocky Mountains* (Chicago: Belford, Clarke and Company, 1889), 559.

12. Doane, "The Report," 8.

13. Doane in Bonney and Bonney, *Battle Drums*, 340.

14. Gunnison, *Rambles Overland*, 39.

15. Doane, "The Report," 29.

16. Hayden, *Preliminary Report*, 121.

17. Norton, *Illustrated*, 13; Rossiter Raymond in Brockett, *Western Empire*, 1259. Other guidebook authors who copied part or all of Doane's report in the geyser basins were Winser, *Great Northwest*; Riley, *Official Guide*; and Chittenden, *Yellowstone Park*.

18. See Thurman Wilkins, *Thomas Moran: Artist of the Mountains* (Norman: University of Oklahoma Press, 1966), and Amy O. Bassford and Fritiof Fryxell, eds., *Home-Thoughts, From Afar* (East Hampton, N.Y.: East Hampton Free Library, 1967).

19. Hayden, *Preliminary Report*, 124 and 122, respectively.

20. Doane, "The Report," 31–32.

21. J. W. Barlow and D. P. Heap, "Report of a Reconnaissance of the Basin of the Upper Yellowstone in 1871," *Sen. Exec. Doc.* 66, 42nd Cong., 2d Sess. (1872), 31.

22. John Gibbon, "The Wonders of the Yellowstone," *Journal of the American Geographical Society of New York* 5, no. 99 (1878): 135–36.

23. Olin D. Wheeler, *Wonderland '96* (St. Paul: Northern Pacific Railroad, 1896), 68.

24. Olin D. Wheeler, *Wonderland '98* (St. Paul: Northern Pacific Railway, 1898), 70.

25. Riley, *Official Guide*, 60–61.

26. J. A. I. Washburn, *To the Pacific and Back* (New York: Sunshine Publishing Company, 1887), 166.

27. R. E. Strahorn, *Enchanted Land*, 14–15.

28. Gerrish, *World's Wonderland*, 208.

29. C. A. Strahorn, *Fifteen Thousand*, 260.

30. Langford, "Wonders, Part One," 12.

31. Riley, *Official Guide*, 57.

32. Reverend Hoyt in Brockett, *Western Empire*, 1241.

33. Hayden, *Preliminary Report*, 83–84.

34. Reverend Hoyt in Brockett, *Western Empire*, 1242.

35. Reverend Talmage in Elia W. Peattie, *A Journey Through Wonderland* (St. Paul: Northern Pacific Railroad, 1890), 33 and 31, respectively.

36. Peattie, *Journey*, 34.

37. Stanley, *Rambles*, 77.

38. Rudyard Kipling, *American Notes: Rudyard Kipling's West*, Arrell Morgan Gibson, ed. (Norman: University of Oklahoma Press, 1979), 112.

39. Caroline L. Paull, "Notes on Yellowstone National Park, June 28–August 4, 1897," Manuscript (Yellowstone Park Research Library, Mammoth Hot Springs, Wyo., 1897), 4.

40. Wingate, *Through the Yellowstone*, 131.

41. Isaac H. Bromley, "The Big Trees and the Yosemite," *Scribner's Monthly* 3, no. 3 (January 1872): 268.

42. Winslow I. Ayer, *Life in the Wilds of America* (Grand Rapids: Central Publishing Company, 1880), 279.

43. Langford, "Wonders, Part One," 13.

44. Langford, "Wonders, Part One," 13.

45. Doane, "The Report," 13.

46. Barlow and Heap, "Reconnaissance," 14.

47. Dunraven, *Great Divide*, 222.

48. Winser, *Great Northwest*, 70.

49. Olin D. Wheeler, *6000 Miles through Wonderland* (St. Paul: Northern Pacific Railroad, 1893), 82.

50. Folsom, "Exploration," 367.

51. Charles Warner, "Editor's Study," in *Old Yellowstone Days*, Paul Schullery, ed. (Boulder: Colorado Associated University Press, 1979), 163.

52. Wheeler, *Wonderland '97*, 53–54.

53. Hayden, *Preliminary Report*, 96.

54. Rossiter W. Raymond, *Camp and Cabin* (New York: Fords, Howard, and Hulbert, 1879), 204.

55. Stephen Jay Gould, "The Creation Myths of Cooperstown," *Natural History* 98, no. 11 (November 1989): 24.

CHAPTER 4

1. William H. Goetzmann, *Exploration and Empire* (New York: W.W. Norton, 1978), 225.

2. Gunnison, *Rambles Overland*, 11.

3. Wilkins, *Thomas Moran*, 63.

4. Langford, "Wonders, Part One," 6–7.

5. Langford, "Wonders, Part Two," 124.

6. Langford, "Wonders, Part Two," 124.

7. Wilkins, *Thomas Moran*, 218–19.

8. Hayden, *Preliminary Report*, 83–84.

9. William Henry Jackson, *Time Exposure* (Albuquerque: University of New Mexico Press, 1986), 200.

10. Goetzmann, *Exploration*, 512.

11. John Gibson, *Great Waterfalls, Cataracts, and Geysers* (London: T. Nelson and Sons, 1887).

12. F. K. Warren, ed., *California Illustrated* (Boston: DeWolfe, Fiske and Company, 1892), and Hezekiah Butterworth, *Zigzag Journeys in the Western States of America* (London: Dean and Son, n.d.).

13. Carrier, *Letters*, 123.

14. O. S. T. Drake, "A Lady's Trip to the Yellowstone Park," *Every Girl's Annual* (London: Hatchard's, 1887), 348.

CHAPTER 5

1. Langford, "Wonders, Part Two," 117.

2. *Scribner's Monthly*, "The Yellowstone National Park," 120.

3. Bradley in Ferdinand V. Hayden, *Sixth Annual Report of the United States Geological Survey of the Territories* (Washington, D.C: GPO, 1873), 239.

4. Chittenden, *Yellowstone Park*, v.

5. Williams, "Vacation Notes," 11.

6. Williams, "Vacation Notes," 11.

7. National Park Service, *Circulars of General Information: The National Parks* (Washington, D.C.: GPO, 1934), 1.

8. Erk, *Merry Crusade*, 119.

9. Thomas D. Murphy, *Three Wonderlands of the American West* (Boston: L. C. Page and Company, 1912), 11.

10. Erk, *Merry Crusade*, 77.

11. Muir, *Our National Parks*, 52.

12. Nellie Meyer Ranney, "1905 Diary Entries Recall Rigors of Wagon Trip to Yellowstone Park: From the Diary of Nellie Meyer Ranney," Charlotte Dehnert, ed., *Wyoming State Journal*, 1 November 1979, n.p.

13. Wingate, *Through the Yellowstone*, 94.

14. C. J. Collins, *Yellowstone National Park* (Omaha: Union Pacific System, 1930), 6.

15. Drake, "A Lady's Trip," 347.

16. Charles W. Stoddard, "In Wonder-Land," *Ave Maria* (Notre Dame, Ind.) 47, no. 7 (August 1898), 202.

17. Kipling, *American Notes*, 98.

18. C. A. Strahorn, *Fifteen Thousand*, 272.

19. Erk, *Merry Crusade*, 66.

20. Mrs. James M. Hamilton, "Through Yellowstone in 1883 with Mrs. James Hamilton," Typewritten manuscript (Yellowstone Research Library, Mammoth Hot Springs, Wyo., 1967), 6.

21. J. L. Stoddard, *Lectures*, 222.

22. Olin D. Wheeler, *Wonderland 1903* (St. Paul: Northern Pacific Railway, 1903), 40.

23. Washburn, *To the Pacific*, 168.

24. Gerrish, *World's Wonderland*, 234–35.

25. Mattoon, "Summer of 1889," 12–13.

26. Wylie, *Yellowstone*, 9.

27. Muir, *Our National Parks*, 56.

28. J. L. Stoddard, *Lectures*, 233.

29. John Sterling Yard in John Francis Kane, ed., *Picturesque America* (New York: Resorts and Playgrounds of America, 1925), 193.

30. A. B. Guptill, *Haynes Guide to Yellowstone Park* (St. Paul: F. Jay Haynes, 1907), 32.

31. J. E. Haynes, *Haynes Guide* (Bozeman, Mont.: Haynes Studios, 1949), 60.

32. Guptill, *Haynes Guide*, 47.

33. Haynes, *1949 Haynes Guide*, 76.

34. Guptill, *Haynes Guide*, 38.

35. Haynes, *1949 Haynes Guide*, 68.

36. Carrie T. McLaughlin, *A Trip to Yellowstone Park in Horse and Buggy Days* (Published privately, 1904), 5.

37. O'Brien, "Future Road," 396.

38. Philetus W. Norris, *Annual Report of the Superintendent of Yellowstone National Park* (Washington, D.C.: GPO, 1880), 20.

39. Winser, *Great Northwest*, 17. These particular hot springs are not—nor were they ever—geysers. At Mammoth Hot Springs, the travertine limestone deposited by the springs is not strong enough to withstand the pressure necessary for a geyser eruption.

40. Kipling, *American Notes*, 93.

41. Wingate, *Through the Yellowstone*, 80.

42. C. F. Gordon Cumming, "The World's Wonderlands in Wyoming and New Zealand," *Overland Monthly* (2d series) 5, no. 25 (January 1885): 11.

43. Doane, "The Report," 14.

44. S. Weir Mitchell, "Through the Yellowstone Park to Fort Custer, Concluding Paper," *Lippincott's Magazine* 26 (July 1880): 33.

45. Norton, *Illustrated*, 14.

46. Norton in R. E. Strahorn, *Rockies and Beyond*, 208.

47. Raymond, *Camp and Cabin*, 189–90.

48. Barlow, "Reconnaissance," 10–11.

49. S. Weir Mitchell, "Through the Yellowstone Park to Fort Custer, Paper Number One," *Lippincott's Magazine* 25 (June 1880): 691–92.

50. Herman Haupt, *The Yellowstone National Park* (New York: J.M. Stoddart, 1883), 45.

51. Gibbon, "Wonders," 118.

52. Union Pacific System, *Geyserland*, 37.

53. For more information on the Hamilton Swimming Pool, see J. E. Haynes, *Haynes New Guide: The Complete Handbook of Yellowstone National Park* (Yellowstone National Park: Haynes Picture Shops, 1934), and Whittlesey, *Place Names*, 143 and 145.

54. Jean C. Sharpe, "A Yellowstone Story 1908–1917: This Is Me and This Is What I Remember," Manuscript (Yellowstone Research Library, Mammoth Hot Springs, Wyo., 1917), 5.

55. Northern Pacific Railroad, *The Way to Wonderland: Yellowstone National Park* (St. Paul: Northern Pacific Railway, 1935), 21–23.

56. W. S. Franklin, "The Yellowstone," *Science* 37, no. 951 (21 March 1913): 447.

57. Gannett, *Sweet Land*, 172–73.

58. William S. Ellis, "The Pitfalls of Success," *National Geographic* 141, no. 5 (May 1972): 628.

59. W. Smith, *Trail*, 38–42.

60. Hayden, *Sixth Annual Report*, 53.

61. N. P. Langford, *The Discovery of Yellowstone Park*, Aubrey L. Haines, ed. (Lincoln: University of Nebraska Press, 1972), 113.

62. Baker, "Marvels," 483.

63. Northern Pacific Railway, *The Way*, 17.

64. Bradley in Hayden, *Sixth Annual Report*, 234.

65. Hugh M. Smith, "Mysterious Acoustic Phenomena in Yellowstone National Park," *Science* 63, no. 1641 (1926): 586.

66. Hiram M. Chittenden, *The Yellowstone National Park* (Cincinnati: Stewart and Kidd Company, 1915), 288–89; Edwin Linton, "Overhead Sounds of the Yellowstone Lake Region," *Science* 71, no. 1836 (1930): 98; and Riley, *Official Guide*, 69, respectively.

67. Jack E. Haynes, *Haynes Guide* (Bozeman, Mont.: Haynes Studios, Inc., 1949), 104.

CHAPTER 6

1. The idea of the misconception of the ideal as it pertains to biological evolution is discussed in Stephen Jay Gould, "Cordelia's Dilemma," *Natural History* 102, no. 2 (February 1991): 21: "The greatest vernacular misconception of evolution views the process as an inexorable machine, working to produce optimal adaptations as best solutions to problems posed by local environments and unconstrained by the whims and past histories of organisms."

2. Susan R. Schrepfer, "Conflict in Preservation: The Sierra Club, Save-the-Redwoods League, and Redwood National Park," *Journal of Forest History* (April 1980): 60.

3. Runte, *Yosemite*, 47.

4. Frederick Law Olmstead in Joseph L. Sax, *Mountains without Handrails* (Ann Arbor: University of Michigan Press, 1980), 24, and Sax, "America's National Parks: Their Principles, Purposes, and Prospects," *Natural History* 85, no. 8 (1976):76; see also Edward Abbey, *Desert Solitaire* (New York: Ballantine Books, 1979).

5. Yi-Fu Tuan, "Space and Place: Humanistic Perspective" in Stephen Gale and Gunnar Olsson, *Philosophy in Geography* (Boston: D. Reidel, 1979), 410.

6. Sax, "Principles, Purposes, and Prospects," 81.

7. Roberts, *Shoshone*, 209.

8. Bartlett, *Wilderness Besieged*.

9. Edwin Kelsey, "Letter to Sister 'G,' December 3, 1898," Letter (Yellowstone Research Library, Mammoth Hot Springs, Wyo., 1898).

10. Carrier, *Letters*, 123.

11. Greater Yellowstone Coalition, *Greater Yellowstone Report* 10, no. 3 (1993).

12. Richard C. Knopf, "Human Experience of Wildlands: A Review of Needs and Policy," *Western Wildlands* 14, no. 3 (1988): 6.

13. Strong, *A Trip*, 79.

14. Wheeler, *Wonderland '96*, 55–56.

15. Schullery, *Mountain Time*, 192.

16. N. P. Langford, Handwritten manuscript of lectures given by N. P. Langford during 1870–71 (Yellowstone Research Library, Mammoth Hot Springs, Wyo., c.1870), 37.

17. Hayden, *Preliminary Report*, 54.

18. The Lions Club, *The Cody Road to Yellowstone Park* (Cody: The Lions Club, 1920), 1.

19. Charles Van Tassell, *"Truthful Lies"* (Bozeman, Mont.: C. Van Tassell, 1913), 23.

20. McLaughlin, *Horse and Buggy Days*, 57.

21. This passage appeared in the 1949 and later editions.

22. Northern Pacific Railway, *The Way*, 49.

23. Langford, "Wonders, Part One," 6–7.

24. Wheeler, *Wonderland '96*, 80.

25. Emerson Hough in Jack E. Haynes, *Haynes New Guide and Motorists' Complete Road Log of Yellowstone National Park* (St. Paul: J.E. Haynes, 1926), 112.

26. McLaughlin, *Horse and Buggy Days*, 87.

27. Thomas R. Vale, "No Romantic Landscapes for Our National Parks?" *Natural Areas Journal* 8, no. 2 (1988): 115–16.

28. Gould, "Creation Myths," 24.

BIBLIOGRAPHY OF ACCOUNTS
USED IN GRAPHS

Anderson, George. "Work of the Cavalry in Protecting Yellowstone National Park." In *Old Yellowstone Days*, edited by Paul Schullery. Boulder: Colorado Associated University Press, 1979.

Andreae, A. "Ueber die künstliche Nachamung des Geysirphänomens." *Neues Jahrbuch für Mineralogie, Geologie und Palaeontologie*, II.Band (Jahrgang 1893): 1–18.

Augspurger, Marie M. *Yellowstone National Park: Historical and Descriptive*. Middletown, Ohio: Naegele-Auer Printing Company, 1948.

Ayer, I. Winslow. *Life in the Wilds of America, and Wonders of the West In and Beyond the Bounds of Civilization*. Grand Rapids: Central Publishing Company, 1880.

Baker, Ray Stannard. "A Place of Marvels: Yellowstone Park As It Now Is." *Century Magazine* 66, no. 4 (1903): 481–91.

Barlow, J. W., and D. P. Heap. "Report of a Reconnaissance of the Basin of the Upper Yellowstone in 1871." *Sen. Exec. Doc. No. 66*, 42nd Cong., 2d sess. (1872): 1–43.

Bassford, A., and Fritiof Fryxell. *Home Thoughts from Afar*. East Hampton, N.Y.: East Hampton Free Library, 1967.

Bauer, Clyde Max. *Yellowstone—Its Underworld*. Washington, D.C.: National Park Service, 1955.

Beadle, J. H. *The Undeveloped West*. Philadelphia: National Publishing Company, 1873.

Beautiful America. *Beautiful America January 1925*. New York: Beautiful America Publishing Corp., 1924.

Bell, Alfred, and Estella Bell (Amanda Bell Spitzer, ed.). "A Wedding Trip to Yellowstone: Summer of 1904." *Tonica (Ill.) News*, 1978. Yellowstone Research Library, Mammoth Hot Springs, Wyo.

Birney, Hoffman. *Roads to Roam*. Philadelphia: Penn Publishing Company, 1930.

Bohlin, K. J. *Genom den Stora Västern.* Stockholm: K.J. Bohlins Förlag, 1893.

Bolin, Luis A. *The National Parks of the United States.* New York: Alfred A. Knopf, 1962.

Borgh, Anna. Letter in *Yellowstone Park News,* No. 5 (December 1988): 2.

Brent, John. *The Empire of the West.* Omaha: Union Pacific Railroad Company, 1910.

Brockett, L. P. *Our Western Empire.* Philadelphia: Bradley and Company, 1881.

Bromley, Isaac H. "The Big Trees and the Yosemite." *Scribner's Monthly* 3, no. 3 (January 1872): 261–77.

Brückmann, Werner. *Du Ferner Westen.* Würzburg: Lothar Sauer-Morhard Verlag, 1948.

Bryant, William Cullen. *Picturesque America, or the Land We Live In.* 2 vols. New York: D. Appleton and Company, 1872.

Bryce, James. *University and Historical Addresses.* New York: Macmillan, 1913.

Buffum, George Washington. Diary-Log of Lumber Wagon Trip from Fort Collins, Colorado, to Yellowstone National Park, Summer of 1885. Yellowstone Research Library, Mammoth Hot Springs, Wyo.

Burroughs, John. "Mit Präsident Roosevelt im Yellowstone = Park." *Kosmos* 6 Jahrgang (1909): 121–27.

———. "The Grand Cañon of the Colorado." *Century* 59, no. 31 (1911): 425–38.

———. "Camping and Tramping with Roosevelt." In *Old Yellowstone Days,* edited by Paul Schullery. Boulder: Colorado Associated University Press, 1979.

Butcher, Devereux. *Exploring Our National Parks and Monuments.* New York: Oxford University Press, 1947.

Butterworth, Hezekiah. *Zigzag Journeys in the Western States of America.* London: Dean and Son, Publishers, 1892.

Campbell, Marius R., et al. *Guidebook of the Western United States.* Part A: The Northern Pacific Route. Washington, D.C.: GPO, 1915.

Campbell, Reau. *Campbell's New Revised Complete Guide and Descriptive Book of the Yellowstone Park.* Chicago: E. M. Campbell, 1909.

———. *Campbell's New Revised Second Edition Complete Guide and Descriptive Book of the Yellowstone Park.* Chicago: H. E. Klamer, 1913.

———. *Campbell's New Revised Third Edition Complete Guide and Descriptive Book of the Yellowstone Park.* Chicago: H. E. Klamer, 1914.

———. *Campbell's New Revised Complete Guide and Descriptive Book of the Yellowstone Park.* Chicago: The Cuneo-Henneberry Company, 1923.

Carpenter, Frank D. *Adventures in Geyserland.* Caldwell, Idaho: Claxton, 1935.

Carrier, Jim. *Letters from the Yellowstone.* Boulder: Roberts Rinehart, Inc., 1987.

Carter, Forest L. "Nick." In *Reminiscences of an Old Yellowstone Ranger between the Years 1921 and 1926.* Grand Marais, Mich.: Grand Sable Publishing Company, 1974.

Chaney, Jack. *Foolish Questions.* Lincoln, Nebr.: Woodruff Press, 1928.

Chapple, Joe. *A' Top O' the World.* Boston: Chapple Publishing Company, Ltd., 1922.

Chatterton, Fenimore, ed. *The State of Wyoming.* Cheyenne: S. A. Bristol Company, 1899.

————. *The State of Wyoming.* Cheyenne: S. A. Bristol Company, 1901.

————. *The State of Wyoming.* Cheyenne: S. A. Bristol Company, 1904.

Chittenden, Hiram Martin. *The Yellowstone National Park: Historical and Descriptive.* Cincinnati: R. Clarke Company, 1895.

————. *The Yellowstone National Park.* Cincinnati: Stewart and Kidd Company, 1915.

————. *Being a Selection from His Unpublished Journals, Diaries and Reports.* Edited by Bruce LeRay. Tacoma: Washington State Historical Society, 1961.

————. *The Yellowstone National Park.* Edited by Richard A. Bartlett. Norman: University of Oklahoma Press, 1964.

Clampitt, J. W. *Echoes from the Rocky Mountains.* Chicago: Belford, Clarke and Company, 1889.

Clawson, Cal C. "The Region of the Wonderful Lake—Yellowstone." *New Northwest* (Deer Lodge, Mont.) (2 and 16 December 1871; 13 and 27 January 1872; 10 and 24 February 1872; 18 May 1872).

Cleland, A. M. *Through Wonderland.* Chicago: Rand McNally, 1910.

Cockhill, Brian, ed. "The Quest of Warren Gillette: Based on the Original Diary." *Montana* 22, no. 3 (Summer 1972): 12–30.

Cook, Charles W., David E. Folsom, and William Peterson. *The Valley of the Upper Yellowstone.* Edited by Aubrey L. Haines. Norman: University of Oklahoma Press, 1965.

Cook, Joel. *America: Picturesque and Descriptive.* 3 vols. Philadelphia: Henry J. Coastes and Company, 1900.

Collins, C. J. *Yellowstone National Park.* Omaha: Union Pacific System, 1930.

Corthell, N. E. *A Family Trek to the Yellowstone.* Laramie: Laramie Printing Company, 1928.

Cox, James. *My Native Land.* St. Louis: Blair Publishing Company, 1888.

————. *Our Own Country.* St. Louis: The National Company, 1894.

Craighead, Karen, and Derek Craighead. "A Walk through the Wilderness." *National Geographic* 141, no. 5 (May 1972): 579–603.

Credner, H. "Der National-Park am Yellowstone." *Geographischer Zeitschrift* 1 (1895): 79–89.

Cruikshank, Margaret Andrews. "A Lady's Trip to Yellowstone in 1883: 'Earth Could Not Furnish Another Such Sight.' " Edited by Lee H. Whittlesey. *Montana* 39, no. 1 (winter 1989): 2–15.

Cumming, C. F. Gordon. "The World's Wonderlands in Wyoming and New Zealand." *Overland Monthly* (2d Series) 5, no. 25 (January 1885): 1–13.

Cundall, Alan W., and Herbert T. Lystrup. *Yellowstone National Park*. West Yellowstone, Mont.: Hamilton Stores, 1969.

Dexter, Mary Reeves. Handwritten letters dated 28 July, 30 July, and 2 August 1889, in Special Collections, Montana State University Library, Bozeman, Mont.

Dickey, Emerson. Excerpts from Journal, July 1932. Yellowstone Research Library, Mammoth Hot Springs, Wyo.

Doane, Gustavus C. "The Report of Lieutenant Gustavus C. Doane upon the So-called Yellowstone Expedition of 1870." *Sen. Exec. Doc. No. 51*, 41st Cong. 3d. Sess. (1871): 1–40.

Donaldson, Rose Simon. "My First Trip to Yellowstone Park, 1925." Yellowstone Research Library, Mammoth Hot Springs, Wyo.

Douglass, Irwin B. "Notes of a Summer Naturalist, 1936–1939." Handwritten notes in Yellowstone Research Library, Mammoth Hot Springs, Wyo.

Drake, O. S. T. "A Lady's Trip to the Yellowstone Park." *Every Girl's Annual*. London: Hatchard's, 1887.

Dumbell, K. E. M. *California and the Far West*. New York: James Pott and Company, 1914.

Dunraven, Earl of. *The Great Divide*. London: Chatto and Windus, Piccadilly, 1876.

Editors of *Garden and Forest*. "Editorial." *Garden and Forest* 1 (4 April 1888): 75.

———. "Protection of the Yellowstone Park." *Garden and Forest* 3 (10 December 1890): 593.

———. "Yellowstone National Park." *Garden and Forest* 4, no. 199 (16 December 1891): 589–90.

———. "The Yellowstone Park Company." *Garden and Forest* 5, no. 210 (2 March 1892): 98.

———. "Editorial Note." *Garden and Forest* 5, no. 218 (9 March 1892): 120.

———. "The Boundaries of Yellowstone Park." *Garden and Forest* 5, no. 222 (25 May 1892): 241.

———. "The Yellowstone National Park." *Garden and Forest* 7, no. 319 (4 April 1894): 131.

———. "Yellowstone Park." *Garden and Forest* 7, no. 321 (18 April 18 1894): 151–52.

Editors of *Overland Monthly*. "A Ten Minute Trip through Yellowstone Park." *Overland Monthly* 70, no. 2 (July 1917): 101–12.

Editors of *Scribner's Monthly*. "The Yellowstone National Park." *Scribner's Monthly* 4, no. 1 (May 1872): 120–21.

Edwards, Guy D. "Yellowstone National Park." *Montana Resources and Opportunities Edition of 1933* 7, no. 4 (1933): 37–38.

Ehrlich, Gretel. "The Volcano Sleeps as We Play." *Traveler* (August 1991): 100–105, 114.

Ellis, William S. "The Pitfalls of Success." *National Geographic* 141, no. 5 (May 1972): 616–31.

Ellsworth, Fred W. "Through Yellowstone Park with the American Institute of Banking." *Moody Magazine* 14, no. 5 (1912): 366–75.

Erk, Edmund Frederick. *A Merry Crusade to the Golden Gate*. Akron, Ohio: The Werner Company, 1906.

Everts, Truman C. "Thirty-Seven Days of Peril." *Contributions to the Historical Society of Montana* 5 (1904): 395–427.

Faris, John T. *Roaming American Playgrounds*. New York: Farrar and Rinehart, Inc., 1934.

Fennell, James Carson. "In the Yellowstone Park." *The California Illustrated Magazine* 2, no. 3 (August 1892): 348–63.

Fenneman, N. M. "The Yellowstone National Park." *Journal of Geography* 11 (June 1913): 314–20.

Ferris, W. A. *Life in the Rocky Mountains 1830–1835*. Edited by Paul C. Phillips. Denver: Old West Publishing Company, 1940.

Folsom, David E. "The Folsom-Cook Exploration of the Upper Yellowstone in the Year 1869." *Contributions to the Historical Society of Montana* 5(1904): 348–69.

Fountain, Paul. *The Eleven Eaglets of the West*. London: John Murray, 1906.

Franklin, W. S. "The Yellowstone." *Science* 37, no. 951 (21 March 1913): 446–47.

Frazer, Elizabeth. "The Last Wilderness." *Saturday Evening Post* (24 January 1920): 14–15, 141, 145, 149, 153, 156.

Freeman, Lewis R. *Down the Yellowstone*. London: William Heinemann Ltd., 1923.

Frost, Ned. "Going through the Park." *Saturday Evening Post* (30 March 1929): 35–37, 121, 124, 127.

Gannett, Henry. *North America*. Vol. 2: The United States. London: Edward Stanford, 1898.

Gannett, L. *Sweet Land.* Garden City, N.Y.: Doubleday, Doran and Company, Inc., 1934.

Garvens-Garvensburg, Wolfgang von. "Wild im Yellowstone-Park." *Kosmos* 7 (1910): 52–54.

Gates, Charles H. *Yellowstone National Park, Alaska and the White Pass.* Toledo, Ohio: Franklin Printing and Engraving Company, 1903.

Geikie, Archibald. *Geological Sketches at Home and Abroad.* New York: Macmillan, 1892.

Gerrish, Theodore. *Life in the World's Wonderland.* Biddleford, Maine (Published privately), 1887.

Gibbon, John. "The Wonders of the Yellowstone." *Journal of the American Geographical Society of New York* 5, no. 99 (September 1873): 112–37.

Gibson, John. *Great Waterfalls, Cataracts, and Geysers.* London: T. Nelson and Sons, 1887.

Grant, Roland Dwight. "Changes in the Yellowstone Park." *Bulletin of the American Geographical Society* 40, no. 5 (January 1908): 277–82.

Gray, John S. "Trials of a Trailblazer: P. W. Norris and Yellowstone." *Montana Magazine of Western History* 22, no. 3 (summer 1972): 54–63.

Grinnell, George Bird. *The Passing of the Great West.* Edited by John F. Reiger. New York: Winchester Press, 1972.

Gunnison, Almon. *Rambles Overland.* Boston: Universalist Publishing House, 1884.

Guptill, A. B. *Practical Guide to Yellowstone National Park.* St. Paul: Pioneer Press, 1890.

———. *A Ramble in Wonderland.* St. Paul: Northern Pacific Railroad, 1892.

———. *Yellowstone Park Guide.* St. Paul: H.L. Collins Company, 1894.

———. *Haynes Guide to Yellowstone Park.* St. Paul: H.L. Collins Company, 1900.

———. *Haynes Guide to the Yellowstone Park.* St. Paul: Pioneer Press, 1907.

———. *Haynes Guide to the Yellowstone Park.* St. Paul: Pioneer Press, 1908.

Hague, Arnold. "Yellowstone National Park." *American Forestry* 19, no. 5 (1913): 300–317.

Hamilton, Mrs. James M. "Through Yellowstone in 1883 with Mrs. James Hamilton." Typewritten manuscript. Yellowstone Research Library, Mammoth Hot Springs, Wyo.

Harrison, Carter H. *A Summer's Outing and The Old Man's Story.* Chicago: Donohue, Henneberry and Company, 1891.

Hassell, Richard Burton. "A Trip to the Yellowstone 49 Years Ago." Yellowstone Research Library, Mammoth Hot Springs, Wyo., 1928.

Hatch, Rufus. A Summer Souvenir: "Uncle Rufus" and "Ma." The New Northwest, 1882.

Hatfield, W. F. "Geyserland and Wonderland": A View and Guidebook of the Yellowstone National Park. St. Anthony, Idaho: W. F. Hatfield, 1905.

Haupt, Herman. The Yellowstone National Park. New York: J.M. Stoddart, 1883.

Hayden, Ferdinand V. Preliminary Report of the U.S. Geological Survey of Montana and Portions of Adjacent Territories; Being a Fifth Annual Report of Progress. Washington, D.C.: GPO, 1872.

———. "The Wonders of the West—II." Scribner's Monthly 3, no. 4 (February 1872): 388–96.

———. Sixth Annual Report of the United States Geological Survey of the Territories. Washington, D.C.: GPO, 1873.

———. "Address of Dr. F. V. Hayden, U.S. Geologist: The Great West and the Scenery of Our National Parks, 15 April 1874." Journal of the American Geographical Society of New York 6, no. 48 (1876): 196–211.

———. "The Yellowstone Park." In The Pacific Tourist, edited by F. E. Shearer. New York: Adams and Bishop, 1879.

———. The Great West. Bloomington, Ill: Charles R. Brodix, 1880.

———. Twelfth Annual Report of the U.S. Geological and Geographical Survey of the Territories. Washington, D.C.: GPO, 1883.

Haynes, F. Jay. Haynes Official Guide: Yellowstone National Park. St. Paul: Pioneer Company, 1912.

Haynes, Jack E. Haynes Guide: The Complete Handbook. St. Paul: J.E. Haynes, 1916.

———. The Motorists' Complete Road Log of Yellowstone National Park. St. Paul: J.E. Haynes, 1920.

———. Haynes New Guide and Motorists' Complete Road Log of Yellowstone National Park. St. Paul: J.E. Haynes, 1921.

———. Haynes New Guide and Motorists' Complete Road Log of Yellowstone National Park. St. Paul: J.E. Haynes, 1926.

———. Haynes New Guide and Motorists' Complete Road Log of Yellowstone National Park. Yellowstone Park, Wyo.: Haynes Picture Shops, 1929.

———. Haynes New Guide: The Complete Handbook of Yellowstone National Park. Yellowstone National Park: Haynes Picture Shops, Inc., 1934.

———. Haynes Guide. Yellowstone Park, Wyo.: Haynes, Inc., 1939.

———. "The First Winter Trip through Yellowstone National Park." *Annals of Wyoming* 14, no. 2 (1942): 88–97.

———. *Haynes Guide.* Yellowstone Park, Wyo.: Haynes, Inc., 1946.

———. *Haynes Guide.* Bozeman, Mont.: Haynes Studios, Inc., 1949.

———. *Haynes Guide.* Bozeman, Mont.: Haynes Studios, Inc., 1952.

———. *Haynes Guide.* Bozeman, Mont.: Haynes Studios, Inc., 1955.

———. *Haynes Guide.* Bozeman, Mont.: Haynes Studios, Inc., 1957.

———. *Haynes Guide.* Bozeman, Mont.: Haynes Studios, Inc., 1958.

Hedges, Cornelius. "Journal of Judge Cornelius Hedges." *Contributions to the Historical Society of Montana* 5 (1904): 370–94.

Heuschkel, Julius, E. George Markin, Glenn F. Muchow, Leverett G. Richards, and Frank B. Wisner. "Yellowstone 1925." Photo album with captions in Yellowstone Research Library, Mammoth Hot Springs, Wyo.

Hochstetter, Ferdinand von. *Neu = Seeland.* Stuttgart, Germany: Cotta'scher Verlag, 1863.

Holmes, Burton. *The Burton Holmes Lectures.* Battle Creek, Mich.: The Little-Preston Company, Limited, 1901.

Hough, Emerson. "An Appreciation of Yellowstone National Park." In *National Park Service Series.* U.S. Railroad Administration's bound collection of thirteen pamphlets, 1919.

———. *Maw's Vacation.* St. Paul: Haynes Picture Shops, 1929.

———. "Forest and Stream's Yellowstone Park Game Exploration." In *Old Yellowstone Days,* edited by Paul Schullery. Boulder: Colorado Associated University Press, 1979.

Hoyt, Colgate. " 'Roughing It Up the Yellowstone to Wonderland': An Account of a Trip through the Yellowstone Valley in 1878." Edited by Carroll Van West. *Montana Magazine of Western History* 36, no. 2 (spring 1986): 22–35.

Hyde, John. "A Description of the Country Traversed by the Northern Pacific Railroad." In *Wonderland; or Alaska and the Inland Passage,* edited by F. Schwatka. St. Paul: Northern Pacific Railroad, 1886.

———. *Wonderland; or the Pacific Northwest and Alaska.* St. Paul: Northern Pacific Railroad, 1888.

James, George Wharton. *Our American Wonderlands.* Chicago: A. C. McClurg & Co., 1915.

Jeffers, Le Roy. *The Call of the Mountains.* New York: Dodd, Mead and Company, 1923.

Johnson, Clifton. *Highways and Byways.* New York: Macmillan Company, 1910.

Johnson, Mrs. Edward H. "Diary of a Trip through Yellowstone Park, 1905." Typewritten manuscript at Yellowstone Park Research Library, Mammoth Hot Springs, Wyo.

Jones, O. T. "In the Yellowstone with Princeton." *Nature* 123, no. 3109 (1929): 852–55.

Jones, William A. *Report upon the Reconnaissance of Northwestern Wyoming Including Yellowstone National Park Made in the Summer of 1873.* Washington, D.C.: GPO, 1875.

Kane, John Francis, ed. *Picturesque America.* New York: Resorts and Playgrounds of America, 1925.

Kelsey, Edwin. Letter to Sister "G," 3 December 1898. Yellowstone Research Library, Mammoth Hot Springs, Wyo.

Kenney, R. D. *From Geyserdom to Show-me Land.* Clyde Park, Mont: R.D. Kenney, 1926.

Kipling, Rudyard. *American Notes.* Edited by Arrell Morgan Gibson. Norman: University of Oklahoma Press, 1891.

———. In *Old Yellowstone Days,* edited by Paul Schullery. Boulder: Colorado Associated University Press, 1979.

Kirk, Henry A. "Sixty Days to and in Yellowstone Park." Edited by Daniel Y. Meschter. *Annals of Wyoming* 44, no. 1 (spring 1972): 5–23.

Kronen, May. "Trip to the Yellowstone National Park, July and August 1907." Typewritten manuscript in possession of family.

Langford, Nathaniel P. "The Wonders of the Yellowstone, Part One." *Scribner's Monthly* 2, no. 1 (May 1871): 1–17.

———. "The Wonders of the Yellowstone, Part Two." *Scribner's Monthly* 2, no. 2 (June 1871): 113–29.

———. "The Ascent of Mount Hayden." *Scribner's Monthly* 6, no. 2 (June 1873): 129–57.

———. *The Discovery of Yellowstone Park.* Edited by Aubrey L. Haines. Lincoln: University of Nebraska Press, 1972.

Lawrence, O. C. "The Old and the New." Typewritten account of travel to Yellowstone National Park in 1909 and 1938. Special Collections, Montana State University Library, Bozeman, Mont.

Leclercq, Jules. *La Terre des Merveilles.* Paris: Librairie Hachette et Cie, 1886.

Leslie, Mrs. Frank. *California: A Pleasure Trip from Gotham to the Golden Gate.* New York: G.W. Carleton and Company, 1877.

Lincoln, Andrew Carey. *Motorcycle Chums in Yellowstone Park*. Chicago: M.A. Donohue and Company, 1913.

Linton, Edwin. "Overhead Sounds of the Yellowstone Lake Region." *Science* 71, no. 1836 (1930): 97–99.

Lohse, Joyce B. *A Yellowstone Savage*. Colorado Springs: J.D. Charles Publishing, 1988.

Ludlow, William. *Report of a Reconnaissance from Carroll, Montana Territory, on the Upper Missouri, to the Yellowstone National Park, and Return, Made in the Summer of 1875*. Washington, D.C.: GPO, 1876.

Marron, Carol. *Yellowstone*. Mankato, Minn.: Crestwood House, 1988.

Marston, Edward. *Frank's Ranche or My Holiday in the Rockies*. London: Sampson Low, Marston, Searle, and Rivington, 1886.

Marx, George S. "Yellowstone Park." In *The State of Wyoming*, edited by Charles W. Burdick. Cheyenne: Sun-Leader Printing House, 1898.

Mattoon, A. M. "The Yellowstone National Park, Summer of 1889." Handwritten journal. Yellowstone Research Library, Mammoth Hot Springs, Wyo.

McElrath, Thomson P. *The Yellowstone Valley*. St. Paul: The Pioneer Press, 1880.

McLaughlin, Carrie Todd. *A Trip to Yellowstone Park in Horse and Buggy Days*. Published privately, 1943.

Melbo, Irving R. *Our Country's National Parks*. Indianapolis: Bobbs-Merrill, 1941.

Mitchell, S. Weir. "Through the Yellowstone Park to Fort Custer. Paper Number One." *Lippincott's Magazine* 25 (June 1880): 688–704.

———. "Through the Yellowstone Park to Fort Custer. Concluding Paper." *Lippincott's Magazine* 26 (July 1880): 29–41.

Montana Bureau of Agriculture, Labor and Industry. *"The Treasure State" Montana and Its Magnificent Resources 1898*. Helena: Independent Publishing Company, 1899.

———. *Montana Resources and Opportunities Edition* 3, no. 2. Helena: Naegele Printing Company, 1928.

Montana Department of Agriculture and Publicity. *The Resources and Opportunities of Montana*. Helena: Independent Publishing Company, 1914.

———. *Resources and Opportunities of Montana*. Helena: Independent Publishing Company, 1918.

———. *Resources of Montana*. Helena: Independent Publishing Company, 1919.

———. *Resources of Montana*. Helena: Independent Publishing Company, 1920.

Montana Department of Publicity of the Bureau of Agriculture, Labor and Industry. *Montana*. Helena: Independent Publishing Company, 1909.

————. *Montana.* Helena: Independent Publishing Company, 1912.

Montana World's Fair Commission. *Montana the Treasure State.* St. Louis: Con. P. Curran Printing Company, 1904.

Muench, Joyce, and Josef Muench. *Along Yellowstone and Grand Teton Trails.* New York: Hastings House, 1949.

Muir, John. *Our National Parks.* Madison: The University of Wisconsin Press, 1981.

Murphy, Thomas D. *Three Wonderlands of the American West.* Boston: L.C. Page and Company, 1912.

Mushbach, J. E. "Diary of J. E. Mushbach, 1878." Handwritten manuscript. Yellowstone Research Library, Mammoth Hot Springs, Wyo.

National Park Service. *General Information Circulars: National Parks and Monuments 1918.* Washington, D.C.: GPO, 1918.

————. "The National Parks, Season of 1920–1927." *Rules and Regulations.* Washington, D.C.: GPO, 1920–1927.

————. *Circulars of General Information: The National Parks 1928.* Washington, D.C.: GPO, 1928.

————. *Circulars of General Information: The National Parks.* Washington, D.C.: GPO, 1934.

————. *Circulars of General Information: The National Parks.* Washington, D.C.: GPO, 1939.

————. *Circulars of General Information: The National Parks.* Washington, D.C.: GPO, 1940.

Norris, Philetus W. *Annual Report of the Superintendent of Yellowstone National Park.* Washington, D.C.: GPO, 1880.

————. *Calumet of the Coteau.* Philadelphia: J.B. Lippincott and Company, 1884.

Northern Pacific Railroad. *The Climate, Soil and Resources of the Yellowstone Valley.* St. Paul: Pioneer Press, 1882.

————. *The Land of Geysers.* St. Paul: Northern Pacific Railway, 1909.

Northern Pacific Railway. *The Way to Wonderland: Yellowstone National Park.* St. Paul: Northern Pacific Railway, 1935.

Northern Pacific Railway and Burlington Route. *Magic Yellowstone.* St. Paul: Northern Pacific Railway, 1933.

Northern Pacific Railway Company. *Yellowstone National Park.* Minneapolis: Bloom Brothers Company, n.d.

Norton, Harry J. *Wonderland Illustrated; or, Horseback Rides through the Yellowstone National Park.* Virginia City, Mont.: Harry J. Norton, 1873.

Olmstead, Frederick Law. "The Yosemite Valley and the Mariposa Big Trees." Edited by Laura Roper. In *Landscape Architecture* 43, no. 1 (1952): 14–23.

Osmond, Mable Cross. "Memories of a Trip through Yellowstone Park in 1874." Typewritten copy of the original manuscript at Yellowstone Research Library, Mammoth Hot Springs, Wyo.

Owen, William O. "The First Bicycle Tour of the Yellowstone National Park." *Outing* (June 1891): 191–95.

Panton, Samuel P. "Surveying in Yellowstone National Park, 1882." *Montana* 36, no. 2 (spring 1986): 72–76.

Paull, Caroline L. "Notes on Yellowstone National Park, June 28–August 4, 1897." Manuscript at Yellowstone Research Library, Mammoth Hot Springs, Wyo.

Peattie, Elia W. *A Journey through Wonderland.* St. Paul: Northern Pacific Railroad, 1890.

Pierce, Flora Chase. Letter dated 8 August 1897. Yellowstone Park Research Library, Mammoth Hot Springs, Wyo.

Pierrepont, Edward. *Fifth Avenue to Alaska.* New York: G.P. Putnam's Sons, 1884.

Price, Rose Lambert. *A Summer in the Rockies.* London: Sampson Low, Marston and Company, Ltd., 1898.

Quick, Herbert. *Yellowstone Nights.* Indianapolis: Bobbs-Merrill, 1911.

Quinn, Vernon. *Beautiful America.* New York: Frederick A. Stokes Company, 1923.

Raftery, John H. *A Miracle in Hotel Building.* Mammoth Hot Springs, Wyo.: Yellowstone Park Company, 1912.

———. "Historical Sketch of Yellowstone National Park." *Annals of Wyoming* 15, no. 2 (April 1943): 101–32.

Ranney, Nellie Meyer. "Diary Entries Recall Rigors of Wagon Trip to Yellowstone Park. From the Diary of Nellie Meyer Ranney." Edited by Charlotte Dehnert. *Wyoming State Journal,* 1 November 1979.

Raymond, Rossiter. *Camp and Cabin.* New York: Fords, Howard, and Hulbert, 1880.

Reik, Henry Ottridge. *A Tour of America's National Parks.* New York: E.P. Dutton and Company, 1920.

Remington, Frederic. In *Old Yellowstone Days,* edited by Paul Schullery. Boulder: Colorado Associated University Press, 1979.

Richardson, James. *Wonders of the Yellowstone.* New York: Scribner, Armstrong, and Company, 1873.

———. *Wonders of the Yellowstone Region.* London: Blackie and Son, Paternoster Buildings, E. C., 1876.

Riley, W. C. *Official Guide to the Yellowstone National Park*. St. Paul: W. C. Riley, 1889.

Roberts, Edwards. *Shoshone and Other Western Wonders*. New York: Harper and Brothers, 1888.

Rodenbaugh, Theo. F. *From Everglade to Cañon with the Second Dragoons*. New York: D. Van Nostrand, 1875.

Rolfe, Mary A. *Our National Parks*. Book 2. New York: Benj. H. Sanborn and Company, 1928.

Roosevelt, Theodore. "Wilderness Reserves: The Yellowstone National Park." In *Old Yellowstone Days*, edited by Paul Schullery. Boulder: Colorado Associated University Press, 1979.

Roylance, Ward J. *Rainbow Roads Guide to Highways 91, 89, and 191*. Salt Lake City: Rainbow Roads, 1953.

Russell, Osborne. *Journal of a Trapper 1834–1843*. Edited by Aubrey L. Haines. Lincoln: University of Nebraska Press, 1965.

Rutgers, Lispenard. *On and Off the Saddle*. New York: G.P. Putnam's Sons, 1894.

Scharff, Robert. *Yellowstone and Grand Teton National Parks*. New York: David McKay Company, Inc., 1966.

Scharr, Barbara Ann. "The Wonderland of Today." *Montana Resources and Opportunities Edition, 1928* (Department of Agriculture, Labor and Industry) 1, no. 2: 209–12.

Scholly, Dan R. *Guardians of the Yellowstone*. New York: William Morrow, 1991.

Schullery, Paul. *Mountain Time*. New York: Simon and Schuster, 1988.

Schwatka, Frederick. *Wonderland*. St. Paul: Northern Pacific Railroad, 1886.

Sharpe, Jean C. "A Yellowstone Story, 1908–1917: This Is Me and This Is What I Remember." Manuscript at Yellowstone National Research Library, Mammoth Hot Springs, Wyo.

Skinner, M. P. *The Yellowstone Nature Book*. Chicago: A.C. McClurg and Company, 1924.

———. *Bears in the Yellowstone*. Chicago: A.C. McClurg and Company, 1925.

Smith, Hugh M. "Mysterious Acoustic Phenomena in Yellowstone National Park." *Science* 63, no. 1641 (1926): 586–87.

Smith, Huntington. "Tourists Who Act Like Pigs." *Saturday Evening Post* (30 May 1953): 36–37, 80, 82–84.

Smith, Wallace. *On the Trail in Yellowstone*. New York: G.P. Putnam's Sons, 1924.

Stanley, Edwin J. *Rambles in Wonderland*. New York: D. Appleton and Company, 1880.

Steel, Byron. *Let's Visit Our National Parks*. New York: Robert M. McBride and Company, 1947.

Steele, David M. *Going Abroad Overland*. New York: G.P. Putnam Sons, 1917.

Stewart, Donald C. *My Yellowstone Years*. Fowlerville, Mich.: Wilderness Adventure Books, 1989.

Stoddard, Charles Warren. "In Wonder-Land." *Ave Maria* (Notre Dame, Ind.) 47, no. 6 (6 August 1898): 172–75.

————. "In Wonder-Land." *Ave Maria* 47, no. 7 (13 August 1898): 200–203.

————. "In Wonder-Land." *Ave Maria* 47, no. 8 (20 August 1898): 237–41.

————. "In Wonder-Land." *Ave Maria* 47, no. 9 (27 August 1898): 257–61.

————. "In Wonder-Land." *Ave Maria* 47, no. 10 (3 September 1898): 295–99.

————. "In Wonder-Land." *Ave Maria* 47, no. 11 (10 September 1898): 326–30.

Stoddard, John L. *John L. Stoddard's Lectures*. Vol. 10. Boston: Balch Brothers Company, 1898.

Story, Isabelle F. *Glimpses of Our National Parks*. Washington, D.C.: GPO, 1941.

Strahorn, Carrie Adell. *Fifteen Thousand Miles by Stage*. New York: G.P. Putnam's Sons, 1911.

Strahorn, Robert E. *The Enchanted Land*. Omaha: New West Publishing Company, 1881.

————. *To the Rockies and Beyond*. Chicago: Belford, Clarke and Company, 1881.

Strong, William Emerson. *A Trip to the Yellowstone National Park*. Edited by Richard A. Bartlett. Norman: University of Oklahoma Press, 1968.

Sutton, Ann, and Myron Sutton. *Yellowstone: A Century of the Wilderness Idea*. New York: Chanticleer Press, 1972.

Sweet, Elnathan. "Horseback in Yellowstone Park." *Country Life in America* 2 (1 June 1912): 88–89.

Synge, Georgina M. *A Ride through Wonderland*. London: Sampson Low, Marston, and Company, 1892.

Taylor, Bayard. *At Home and Abroad*. New York: G.P. Putnam, 1859.

Taylor, Charles M. *Touring Alaska and the Yellowstone*. Philadelphia: George W. Jacobs and Company, 1901.

Taylor, E. O. "Notes of a Trip to Yellowstone National Park, 1885." Handwritten diary in Special Collections, Montana State University, Bozeman, Mont.

Thane, Eric. *The Majestic Land: Peaks, Parks and Prevaricators of the Rockies and Highland Northwest*. Indianapolis: Bobbs-Merrill, 1950.

Thayer, William M. *Marvels of the New West*. Norwich, Conn.: Henry Bill Publishing Company, 1891.

Tilden, Freeman. *The Fifth Essence*. Washington, D.C.: The National Park Trust Fund Board, 1954.

Topping, E. S. *Chronicles of the Yellowstone*. St. Paul: Pioneer Press Company, 1883.

Trager, Martelle. *National Parks of the Northwest*. New York: Dodd, Mead and Company, 1939.

Trumbull, Walter. "The Washburn Yellowstone Expedition. Number One." *Overland Monthly* 6, no. 5 (May 1871): 431–37.

———. "The Washburn Yellowstone Expedition. Number Two." *Overland Monthly* 6, no. 6 (June 1871): 489–96.

Turpin, Frances Lynn. "A Trip through Yellowstone Park, 1895." Typewritten manuscript in Special Collections, Montana State University Library, Bozeman, Mont.

Turrill, Gardner Stilson. *A Tale of the Yellowstone*. Jefferson, Iowa: G. S. Turrill Publishing Company, 1901.

Tweedy, Frank. "The Forests of Yellowstone National Park." *Garden and Forest* 1 (9 May 1888): 129–30.

Union Pacific System. *Geyserland*. Omaha: W. H. Murrary, 1924.

United States Railroad Administration. *Yellowstone National Park*. Chicago: Rand McNally, 1919.

Van Tassell, Charles. *"Truthful Lies."* Bozeman, Mont.: C. Van Tassell, 1913.

Victor, Frances Fuller. *The River of the West*. Oakland: Brooks-Sterling Company, 1974.

Vosburgh, Frederick G. "Yellowstone National Park." *America's Wonderland*. Washington, D.C.: National Geographic Society, 1959.

Warner, Charles. In *Old Yellowstone Days*, edited by Paul Schullery. Boulder: Colorado Associated University Press, 1979.

Warren, F. K., ed. *California Illustrated*. Boston: DeWolfe, Fiske and Company, 1892.

Washburn, Henry D. "Report on Mining Statistics West of the Rocky Mountains." *House Exec. Doc. No. 10*, 42d Cong., 1st. Sess. (1871): 213–16.

Washburn, J. A. I. *To the Pacific and Back*. New York: Sunshine Publishing Company, 1887.

Weikert, Andrew J. "Journal of the Tour through the Yellowstone National Park in August and September, 1877." *Contributions to the Historical Society of Montana* 6 (1904): 153–74.

Wheeler, Olin D. *6,000 Miles through Wonderland*. St. Paul: Northern Pacific Railroad, 1893.

————. *Sketches of Wonderland*. St. Paul: Northern Pacific Railroad, 1895.

————. *Wonderland '96*. St. Paul: Northern Pacific Railroad, 1896.

————. *Wonderland '97*. St. Paul: Northern Pacific Railway, 1897.

————. *Wonderland '98*. St. Paul: Northern Pacific Railway, 1898.

————. *Wonderland '99*. St. Paul: Northern Pacific Railway, 1899.

————. *Wonderland 1900*. St. Paul: Northern Pacific Railway, 1900.

————. *Wonderland 1901*. St. Paul: Northern Pacific Railway, 1901.

————. *Wonderland 1902*. St. Paul: Northern Pacific Railway, 1902.

————. *Wonderland 1903*. St. Paul: Northern Pacific Railway, 1903.

————. *Wonderland 1904*. St. Paul: Northern Pacific Railway, 1904.

————. *Wonderland 1905*. St. Paul: Northern Pacific Railway, 1905.

————. *Wonderland 1906*. St. Paul: Northern Pacific Railway, 1906.

White, Alma. *With God in the Yellowstone*. Zarephath, N.J.: Pillar of Fire, 1933.

White, Zillah Pocick. Handwritten letter. Yellowstone Research Library, Mammoth Hot Springs, Wyo., 1986.

Williams, J. E. "Vacation Notes: Summer of 1888 (Through the Yellowstone Park)." *Amherst (Mass.) Record* (26 September 1888): 1–52.

Wingate, George W. *Through the Yellowstone Park on Horseback*. New York: O. Judd Company, 1886.

Winser, Henry J. *The Great Northwest*. New York: G.P. Putnam's Sons, 1883.

————. *The Yellowstone National Park: A Manual for Tourists*. New York: G.P. Putnam's Sons, 1883.

Wister, Owen. "Old Yellowstone Days." *Harper's Monthly Magazine* 172 (1936): 471–81.

————. *Owen Wister Out West*. Edited by Fanny Kemble Wister. Chicago: The University of Chicago Press, 1958.

Wolfe, Thomas. *A Western Journal*. Pittsburgh: University of Pittsburgh Press, 1951.

Wylie, W. W. *Yellowstone National Park*. Kansas City, Mo.: Ramsey, Millett and Hudson, 1882.

Wylie, William H., and Sara King Wiley. *The Yosemite, Alaska, and the Yellowstone*. New York: John Wiley and Sons, 1892.

Yard, Robert Sterling. *The National Parks Portfolio*. Washington, D.C.: GPO, 1917.

Yeager, Dorr G. *Your Western National Parks*. New York: Dodd, Mead and Company, 1947.

Zardetti, Otto. *Westlich! oder Durch den fernen Westen Nord-Amerikas*. Mainz: Verlag von Franz Kirchheim, 1897.

Index

ABOUT THE AUTHOR

Judith L. Meyer was born in Iowa and grew up in Delaware, Ohio. After graduating from Cornell College with a double major in Environmental Studies and German, she attended graduate school in the Ecology Curriculum at the University of North Carolina at Chapel Hill for two years before moving to Yellowstone National Park in 1980 to work as a bilingual tour guide for TW Recreational Services, the park concessioner. In 1983, she returned to the Midwest to study at the University of Wisconsin at Madison, where she met and married her husband, had three children, and completed an M.S. in adult education and a Ph.D. in geography.

Dr. Meyer currently teaches geography at Carthage College in Kenosha, Wisconsin, but will move to the Department of Geography, Geology, and Planning at Southwest Missouri State University in Springfield in January 1997.